FOR BETTER AND GREATER

Solutions For Marriages And Families

Apostle Steve Lyston

Copyright © 2023 Apostle Steve Lyston

Library of Congress Control Number: 2023938386
ISBN: 978-1-7359220-4-1

All rights reserved. No part of this publication may be reproduced,
or transmitted in any form or by any means, electronic or mechanical,
including photocopying, recording, or by any information storage and retrieval system, without prior permission in writing from the
copyright owner.

Edited by: Michelle R. Lyston
Cover Design by: Johann D. A. Williams
Scripture quotations marked "NKJV" are taken from The New King
James Version / Thomas Nelson Publishers, Nashville: Thomas Nelson Publishers. Copyright © 1982. Used by permission. All rights reserved.

This book was printed in Columbia, South Carolina in the United States of America

DEDICATION

This book is dedicated to:

The nuclear family around the globe and to the sanctity of marriage.

My family – Steve, Michelle, Shevado, Hannah & Joshua

The entire RWOMI Family, all its affiliates and partners globally

+

THANK YOU

God – The Father, Jesus Christ – the Son and the Holy Spirit of God, for the continued Divine Revelation.

Bishop Dr. Doris Hutchinson and The RWOMI Watchman Team for your continue support

TABLE OF CONTENTS

		Page
Introduction		
Chapter 1	Reality Check Needed On Relationships	7
Chapter 2	Fixing The Family	20
Chapter 3	Life Is More Than The Economy	26
Chapter 4	Preparing For Marriage	40
Chapter 5	Married People Should Have More Sex	71
Chapter 6	Get Back To Basics	84
Chapter 7	Fathers Leading The Change	94
Chapter 8	Dealing With Incest And Sexual Abuse	107
Chapter 9	More Training For Parents Not Criticisms	133
Chapter 10	Men And Women Of Purpose Arise	148
Chapter 11	The Daily Fight Men Go Through	159
Chapter 12	Wisdom For Healthy Living	166
	Bibliography	

INTRODUCTION

Globally, the nuclear family as we know it is under great threat. Furthermore, the institution of marriage is constantly pressed from every side.

Ephesians 5 gives the instructions that Christian households need to abide by to maintain healthy marriages and families. In fact, Ephesians 5: 28 – 29 says, "In this same way, husbands ought to love their wives as their own bodies. He who loves his wife loves himself. After all, no one ever hated their own body, but they feed and care for their body, just as Christ does the church".

Undoubtedly, if the family and marriages are under attack, then the church and the nation are under attack as strong families not only make a strong community and a strong church, but strong families make a strong nation.

The Scripture above also reminds that if a person is unable to manage their own household, then they will not be able to manage the church, their organization nor the nation.

A person's family life should be used as the number one criterion for public office. Every nation needs to establish a Ministry of Family Affairs/Department of Family Affairs, and every household needs to establish a family altar to pray for the success of families and marriages if they desire to see change at any level.

Chapter 1

REALITY CHECK NEEDED ON RELATIONSHIPS

There are many relationship problems that have been taking place, many of which lead to abuse and death. From time-to-time people come forward and have much to say about these issues but oftentimes we must wonder if they really seek to find out the real root cause in order to truly solve the matter. Domestic violence is one such area of immense concern, but we need to determine the root of this issue to effectively deal with it.

Family is the most important thing in any nation but is given the least attention. Most of the problems in existence today stem from a broken family situation.

Hard Truths To Face

First, we need to address the ever-increasing number of Common-Law Relationships within the nation. Whether we want to accept it or not, Common-Law relationships establish wrong covenants and create un-Godly soul ties which ultimately affect our nation and its growth negatively. It is very disappointing that both the media and the national political hierarchy have turned a blind eye to it. They themselves are married, but they are not encouraging others to do the same. In fact, many encourage common law relationships, but make loud declarations about coming out of poverty. How can we come out of poverty if we are not properly aligned and functioning in proper order?

Second, the abuse of our women has become rampant within our society. However, we must as a nation, realize and accept that abuse is not only meted out to the women in our society. Men are also victims of abuse.

The lack of support for our women in the society drives many of our women into unhealthy relationships with others and of particular interest are the relationships with older men – the "sugar daddies" – who would spend a great deal of money on them. They then dump these older men in favor of relationships with younger men, and in some cases, that leads to murder, or murder/suicide.

Furthermore, the lack of counselors drives many men to seek advice from bartenders and those in prostitution, and some of those women would encourage them to go home and "deal with" their women. Sadly, there are some women who welcome the beatings because it is an indication to them that the men care about them somehow.

It is interesting to note that many of the men who abuse women were themselves abused and their mothers were also abused, as they grew up without their own fathers and were at the mercy of stepfathers or other males in their home.

Solutions

It is critical for every stakeholder within the nation, the political hierarchy and the Church to unite and create programs that will empower and uplift the family in a balanced fashion – that is, both male and female instead of passing laws that are biased against the men, promoting abortion and engaging in other activities that fight against the family as God ordained it.

It is important to create a place of shelter to temporarily house those who are abused and having Spirit-Filled Chaplains who will carry out counseling and rehabilitation.

There needs to be free education extended to deal with the Family, and in particular to teach about Parenting.

Conflict Resolution

A campaign needs to be launched and carried out to deal with those in Common-Law relationships with a view to them getting married or being set on the right path. A separate Ministry Portfolio in the Government that deals directly with Family, where the head of that Ministry is married and can set an example.

There should be tax incentives given for those who are married.

The same marketing approach that is taken to promote the vaccine should be employed to encourage marriage and healthy family relationships. In the same way they spend money, do giveaways and advertisements – should be devoted to building strong families. Invest heavily in eradicating the virus of Common-Law Relationships; censor all news and advertisements that use famous people to promote Common Law relationships and children being born out of wedlock.

Give a Marriage Allowance to all Civil Servants. This will encourage all Civil Servants as well as the Security Personnel; and have a Private Sector initiative to join the fight. It would be one of the biggest transformations in the nation, and also the solution for crime reduction.

Handling Conflict

Conflict is something none of us can avoid. From time to time, we will have conflict in the family, in the Church; in fact, there was even conflict in heaven! The devil is the author of conflict. Conflict brings division, pain, distress and so on.

When conflict arises, it is critical for us to ensure that we deal with conflict with wisdom in order to avoid major damage. God uses conflict as an opportunity to birth or to promote us when we deal with it correctly.

Conflict is an opportunity to bring change; not change of leadership but change of tactics and strategies and leadership styles. Conflict also has the ability to bring reform or restructuring in the Church as is seen in Acts 6. In that Scripture, we see where conflict birthed the ministry or Deacons, which brought great church growth.

The keys to dealing with conflict are:

- Listen to the complaint(s)
- Deliberate and discuss the issues.
- Action and make decisions.
- Avoid Gossiping. If one has a complaint, they must be able to speak in the presence of the person with whom they have the issue.
- Call a time of prayer.
- Follow the leading of the Holy Spirit
- Guard the heart.
- Avoid Pride and Rebellion
- Everything must be settled in Love and Harmony
- Everything must be done decently and in order.
- Exclude selfish desires.

Remember, conflict stops the flow of the Holy Spirit to bring blessing within the organization. (*Matthew 5: 9; Romans 12:*

18) That is why each person must guard their heart and put on the whole armor of God! While it may reveal underlying problems, conflict has the opportunity to bring maturity and to bring the church to the next level.

Remember also, that for church growth, there must be organization and delegation. This is why we need the Holy Spirit for wisdom to solve problems. When we resolve conflict God's way, the entire congregation will be pleased. Never try to avoid a conflict and pretend it isn't there; it will explode and become worse than you anticipated!

We must treat conflict in such a way that it does not negatively affect the congregation or the Pastor/Apostle.

We see in III John 9 – 12, Diotrephes and Demetrius. John showed the church how to be unlike Diotrephes, but instead follow those who had a good report among them. John extended patience. Unlike Apostle Paul and Alexander the Coppersmith (II Timothy 4: 14 – 16) who opposed and resisted God's work. Anyone who opposes and resists Gods work, they must be dealt with quickly.

Conflict allows both sides to examine their hearts and motives.

Types of Conflict

There are 3 different types of conflict:

- Interpersonal - conflict with 2 or 3 persons

- ➤ Intrapersonal - This is internal. It is Self-Desire vs. God's desire/will.

- ➤ Substantive - Conflict on Moral grounds. For example, having to do with the visions, goals and doctrinal belief. This is the worst one, because it undermines the moral integrity of the visionary. People silently rebel against the operation of the church while they spread it to other leaders of their disagreement. This is dangerous, especially in small congregations. It causes pain, church splits and can affect the church for years to come. The church will need to Fast in order to root it out of the church.

Pray that conflict is rooted out!

(Additional Scriptures: Mark 3: 25; Galatians 6: 1 – 5; Proverbs 16: 18 – 19)

Domestic Violence

With the continuous spotlight on Domestic Violence, and the laws being proposed to address the situation, recognize that unless we are completely truthful about this issue, we are simply playing politics.

Many times, blame is levied on the church when domestic violence takes place. Pastors often give the proper advice to one or both parties in the marriage, but the advice is ignored and then the Pastor is either blamed or is accused of trying to break them up.

Before a relationship is formed, and before the Church can say it sanctions a marriage, several things need to be confirmed. They must determine if the union the will of God and then instruct accordingly concerning the Spiritual Protocol they need to follow. Do they:

- ✓ **Have the consent of both sets of parents.**
- ✓ **Have their Pastor(s) consent.**
- ✓ **Were abusive or abused in a past relationship.**

If there is a negative response from the Pastor/Counsellor, some couples refuse to heed the red flags, and go searching for a Pastor/Counselor who will marry them for a price.

Choices

Everything we do in life has to do with the choices we make. Domestic Violence starts with the wrong choices. There are people within society who will tell you that they love "bad men", "gunmen", "rude-boys" and the like, and many of them abuse others as well. If we are going to deal with domestic violence, then we cannot promote promiscuity, common law relationships, marijuana use – medical or otherwise, nor can we promote the argument that we can do whatever we want to do with or to our bodies; because they all have negative consequences. We must get back to Biblical basics and deal with the red flags; otherwise, abuse will reign rampant.

Red Flags

Here are some **Red Flags!**

- When a man tells you that you're going to church too often or try to pull you away from your family.

- When they don't want counseling when something goes wrong.

- When your spouse tells you not to have your own bank account.

- When your husband keeps getting you pregnant regularly in hopes that no one else will want you while he mistreats you.

- When your spouse doesn't want you to work and earn a living just so that they can have control over you financially and otherwise.

- When your spouse is "policing" your phone and keeps telling you that if it wasn't for them, you wouldn't be where you are or have what you have.

Abuse Is Learned Behavior

Abuse is learned based on what the child sees in his/her home. What they learn from parents and from a cartoon character. Abuse should never be treated as a gender issue nor an issue of class. Abuse is even more prevalent at the top, as many in the influential "bracket" engage in abuse, and those on the receiving end can't even speak to anyone about it. Pride and the fear of going back to poverty holds them at ransom. At school, any good teacher can identify the signs of abuse in/on their students.

A person who is not delivered from anger will become a gateway for abuse to enter the home. Deliverance cannot come by way of medication. It must be dealt with Spiritually.

Witchcraft also plays a role in abuse but could not be effective without a pre-existing stronghold – such as, pride, lack of self-control or fear and rejection.

True Love won't propel you to kill someone then kill yourself. When disappointment or infidelity takes places, don't be afraid to walk away; but keep in mind that the Bible also supports separation for reconciliation. There is always life – hope. God will provide even better! Never do anything you will regret. Pray, Fast, and Speak to mature people who qualify to speak into your life.

Domestic Violence And The Army

The army has been very prominent in the media lately regarding domestic violence, not only locally, but it is a common issue internationally. Many cast blame and are taking sides at the gender level; but domestic violence should never be dealt with on the basis of gender. If we are looking at gender, the fact is that more men die than women. It is our responsibility to look at both sides of the story, rather than jumping on one side of the fence.

Core Values

There are many things that cause violence at this level. It stems from economic, social, cultural, and moral behaviors. Parenting also plays a role in the whole thing. It is disappointing when a soldier makes the headlines in such a negative way; but what many don't understand is that soldiers are trained to be emotionally hard. They are trained to take pressure and heavy stress; however, they have also been taught core values – courage, loyalty, respect integrity, commitment, and discipline – and must demonstrate them. The Bible also says that a good soldier should not be distracted or entangle himself with civilian matters but must serve wholeheartedly. (2 Timothy 2: 3 – 4)

Recipe For Disaster

In dealing with domestic violence, we must also look at the things that negatively influence the actions of the soldier, and how we can work together to minimize those influences - the demand on a nation to solve crime and violence, or the demand for soldiers to go to war, for example. One of the things which affects them seriously is the lack of quality time they are able to spend with their families; and it is no secret that the long hours away lead to infidelity on the part of their spouse. So, while they are patrolling out there, somebody else is "patrolling" at (their) home. One of the worst things the soldier can hear is that somebody else is "doing the work", and it is worse when they are being jeered by fellow soldiers.

Soldiers are not girl guides or cub scouts; they are trained to kill. For soldiers, especially those with less than six (6) years of service, being away for long hours doing police duties (which they are not trained to do) along with the personal pressures, is a recipe for disaster.

Actions For Moving Forward

While the government wants to boost security in an effort to increase employment among the youth, they must be careful of how they treat the senior ones, particularly as it relates to retiring soldiers. Without a doubt, there is a serious lack of mentors – youth can't mentor youth. They may have to start calling back those who were honorably discharged in order to bring balance and avoid greater problems.

More time needs to be given to soldiers for family recreation to ease the tension, allow all involved to have peace of mind, less stress and greater productivity. Every now and then an "oil change" is needed.

An experienced RSM (Regimental Sergeant Major) or CSM (Company Sergeant Major) or Platoon Sergeant, must be able to quickly identify when something has gone wrong within the family and act wisely. The army also needs to carefully examine the area of Chaplaincy, and how they can bring a new Spiritual climate to bring a refreshing to them. We cannot allow them to operate without that kind of atmosphere – something that Yoga and the New Age Activities cannot provide. The Chaplain must be one to help the soldiers beyond simply recommending disciplinary action.

Neighbors and family members must be encouraged to report, with proof, any form of domestic violence they know of, to the Officer in Command of the soldier's unit, or to the Military Police or Chaplain without fear that the soldier will be discharged.

Furthermore, there are many soldiers who suffer with PTSD (Post Traumatic Stress Disorder) and who need medical help. There are others who are afraid to re-adjust to civilian life because they don't have much savings, and others don't know how to survive and that has a negative impact on them. So, the private sector, banking sector and government must put more systems in place particularly low-income housing. This will minimize domestic violence.

Instead of hurling negative criticisms, let us work together to preserve life.

Chapter 2

FIXING THE FAMILY

Family is the most important thing within society and the family is broken and abnormal. If we want the economy to be right, first we have to deal with the family. So now, those who were the offended are becoming the offenders. Recognize that this cannot be dealt with by spending thousands per day on rehab counseling sessions, nor with theological or psychological ideologies; neither will be registering them as sex offenders while the real offender is untouchable. What we are dealing with is perversion, and perversion is not an illness, it is a spirit. We cannot fix it while excluding God from our society. Likewise, when someone who is now a priest or a pastor, but who was abused growing up and the situation was left unresolved and without them being healed. When that person is placed over a congregation without being healed, what do we expect? Every category within society has something similar to deal with.

Parenting

We need to get back to basics and start with proper parenting. Parents must create an environment that their children will not be afraid to express themselves when family members or any professional service within society who abuse or try to abuse them. Most play naïve and try to cover it up.

Many parents also try to push their children into certain sports or entertainment in an attempt at fame without realizing the consequences and the dangers that the children are encountering. The parents must discern and know the background of the individuals that will be working with your child. Realize that the moment a child is abused, particularly in that way, then his/her life takes a downward turn and we need to catch that as quickly as possible, as it can seriously affect every relationship they have including marriage.

Parents are the ones with the responsibility of ensuring the protection of their children at all levels. They have to police them and protect them from certain elements including entertainment and social networks.

Prison System

The prison system should be one that rehabilitates, not preparing them to be repeat offenders. Oftentimes they are abused within the prison system. Any prison system that is anti-family and does not allow conjugal visits, we should not support that.

It is critical for the government to ensure that when children are placed in homes of safety or in the custody of the state, those who are in charge should be checked to see if they were themselves abused in the past. If that is found to be so, then that needs to be dealt with before they can deal with the children. Many of them have suffered in this way and we need also to recognize that it is not only girls that are at risk but the boys are even more vulnerable.

Education System

Schools need to make it a part of their system that when there are field trips, parents are given the opportunity to accompany their children on the trips. It should also be mandatory that the heads of the Physical Education department be one male and one female. Furthermore, there should be vigilance in the Daycare and proper checks need to be done on those who are to be the helpers.

Parents also need to ask God's guidance in choosing where and to whom their children are sent, because the effects of this kind of abuse are life-long if left unresolved.

Recognize that pedophilia and such behavior are not psychotic issues to be medicated, it is spiritual.

The Best Parenting Handbook

The family is the first line of government, and with the failing of the family structure globally, parents need and must necessarily use the Best Parenting Handbook – the Bible – as a guide to good parenting.

1. Teach your children to in obedience to both spiritual and biological parents; especially those parents who are Christians. Obedience determines their success and longevity of their lives. (Ephesians 6: 1 – 3)

2. When children fail to honor earthly parents, they will not learn to honor God either. This will bring instability in the family and affect the social fabric of the nation. (Deuteronomy 5: 16)

3. When parents fail to teach their children, the entire nation suffers, and that is what is now causing the spiritual drought now affecting nations. (Exodus 20: 12)

4. Teach your children about sound financial responsibility by teaching them about Tithing and the giving of Offerings.

5. Maintain good communication with your children using God's Word as the number one criteria when training them. Avoid any destructive doctrine or philosophy. Communicate with them at the dinner table, when you're walking or driving, when you are going to bed at night or rising up in the morning! (Deuteronomy 6: 6 – 9)

6. Teach your children the goodness of God daily, as well as the power of prayer! Share your testimony with them.

7. Teach your children how to choose with regard to relationships of all kinds – personal and business. Let them know they are to avoid becoming unequally yoked, and to avoid relationships with people who refuse to serve the same God as they serve. Let them know that the vision of those they want to connect with in relationships must be in line with their vision. (Deuteronomy 23: 8 – 12)

8. Choices are key to success! Choices determine the inheritance of your children.

9. Teach your children to avoid tattoos and sex before marriage. Let them know that their virginity is priceless! Keep them away from perverted music and movies.

10. Teach your children how to obey God's voice daily. (Deuteronomy 28: 1 – 14)

11. Pray a hedge of protection around your children
    – as Job did! (Job 1: 1 – 4)

12. Teach your children about the different roles that each parent plays. For example, the mother nurtures the children, and the father instills discipline. (Proverbs 1: 8 – 9)

13. The father should use the Word of God and allow the Holy Spirit to help him to carry out discipline and their fatherly role.

14.   Declare blessings over your children daily.
        (Colossians 3: 21; Ephesians 6: 4;
        Proverbs 29: 15; Proverbs 13: 24; Proverbs 19:
        18; Proverbs 22: 15)

15.   When parents fail to discipline their children,
    we
        fail and we hate our children. Failure will bring
        shame and disgrace to the family.

Chapter 3

LIFE IS MORE THAN THE ECONOMY

Have you ever stopped to think that if man placed greater value on life than they do the economy, how much better off the world would be?

Every day we wake up we are inundated with the resounding chorus "The Economy! The Economy! The Economy!" Was it the economy that resulted in the COVID-19 pandemic? Was it the economy why so many people died during the pandemic?

Poor Decisions

Mankind continues to make decisions in the name of the economy. Economy seems to be the new god. Any individual government or group that prioritizes the economy in a nation above all else, then there will be failure and chaos and more of what is called "Climate Change".

While the economy was made by God to service and sustain man, God did not create it to be worshiped. He instructed man to take dominion. He even instructed man to have a day of rest unto Him, but because of the economy man cannot even keep the 10 Commandments.

Rebellion

It was man's rebellion against God that caused man to be thrown out of the garden, bringing curses upon mankind.

Jesus Christ had to come to reconcile mankind to God, and even so, man still has not learned the lesson. So, although Jesus dies to restore man, man still rejects God.

What should have been managed by us is now managing us, and we are now becoming slaves of the economy. Hence, we have diverted from the path of true prosperity, fighting for something we cannot carry beyond the natural realm. As a result, people are now dying for want of the basic needs – food, shelter, health, and justice.

When man only focuses on "How wealthy can I get?" or "What can I cut to get greater wealth and expand my profit?" "How much can I hide away for myself?"
Man has shifted from God and has allowed the serpent to lead them. But they must remember that Revelation 12: 9 says, So the great dragon was cast out, that serpent of old, called the Devil and Satan, who deceives the whole world; he was cast to the earth, and his angels were cast out with him.

Therefore, regardless of how wealth man becomes, if Christ is not priority, then there will be a significant waste taking place. The soul will run into problems and that is why we must have fellowship with God.

Destroying The Family

Many have been destroying their families, adding to the brokenness of families within nations. It cannot be that every decision we make is solely about the economy. We put wrong leaders in position, because of the economy and this is why we have poor representation.

The economy goes beyond money management, investments, stocks, bonds, yachts, and private jets. It's all about maintaining the human resources where the family is the first line of government. The family is now broken, and many have been neglected because man has put the economy first.

The Word and The Holy Spirit

There are 2 keys of uttermost importance for man's survival – the Word and the Holy Spirit of God.

The Word symbolizes man's nourishment and sustenance both spiritually and naturally. It also represents cleansing, direction, moral guidance and power to get wealth. The Holy Spirit is man's GPS (God's Positioning System). HE will lead us into the direction the father wants us to go; and He is the only One who leads us through the right way, and into a better relationship with the Father. He opens our eyes to know what it is the priority.

The World's Way

The world's way is about greed. They are not about bringing a cure. Instead, everything they have to offer is about treating symptoms, not finding the root cause.

God has created everything for the benefit of man including the economy and He did not charge us for it. He created the fruit trees, the insects, the Livestock, rivers, fish, then gave us air and sunlight, and all we did was erode it all. We are seeing man destroy everything that God gave to mankind in the name of the economy – mad scientists included.

Where Are We

We are at the stage now where:

- the market is more important than mental health.

- the oceans are being depleted and destroyed for the sake of the market.

- the air has been tampered with and the environment neglected.

- the poor have been neglected and babies slaughtered in the name of the economy.

If we truly care about the economy and you want it to be strong, then we must change our priorities and our ways to avert the calamity ahead.

Financial Literacy Needed

Luke 11: 52 says, "Woe to you lawyers! For you have taken away the key of knowledge. You did not enter in yourselves, and those who were entering in you hindered."
Knowledge changes life and environment. People become poor because there is a set of persons in society that constantly do all they can to hinder knowledge from the poor. They constantly stand at the door to stop the poor from laying hold of the knowledge that can build them up. It is no secret that most of the resources the rich make is off the backs of the poor.

Acquiring knowledge is very expensive and most of the poor cannot afford to access it. Many have turned it into a business, and very few know where or how to search to find it. Sometimes the poor enter transactions with limited information afforded to them, and then it ushers them into debt. However, to the banks, it gives them a foothold into the financial future of such people. For the rich, it is an opportunity to make greater profit. So, to change the environment from poverty to prosperity, the poor first needs to know the private laws that will bring great benefits to the user.

So, in the same way the rich do, we should begin to operate with the mindset of "own nothing control everything". Understand that whatever is in your name can be taken away. Also, we need to understand the concept of *eminent domain*.

We also need to know what expatriate investors know, and how they benefit. We need to seek to understand how they qualify for assistance whether *or not* they have suffered a loss, when the poor merely gets a care package.

The Traits of a Godly Billionaire

There is nothing wrong with money; it is the love of money that is the root of all evil. So, there is nothing wrong with having money. As long as we are not possessed with the spirit of mammon, then we are okay.

- ✓ Godly billionaires look to God as their source, not to man. Their trust is in God, hence, in time of famine. Godly billionaires understand the poor. They understand prayer and fasting and their importance to growth, development and expansion. For example, the Ezra Fast. They understand the power and value of Tithing and they know the benefits of giving to the poor to maintain their wealth and riches.

- ✓ Godly billionaires know the benefits and blessings of hiring good staff who are Christians and will do everything to keep them.

- ✓ Godly billionaires will pay decent wages and will not steal from or shortchange their staff members. They pay them on time because they understand biblical principles. They also use the Bible, and the instruction of the Holy Spirit to make decisions when terminating staff, they always do it in love and in accordance with the Word of God. (Philippians 2: 30)

- ✓ They don't show partiality in the business place; they treat all with fairness (Leviticus 19: 15) They understand fair income (Leviticus 19: 13, James 5). They refuse to rob hired servants or aliens. (Deuteronomy 24: 14 – 15). There are many organizations that are robbing the wages of the poor, and most organizations are now receiving a curse as a result. When they get low wages, banks and other institutions extract most if not all of the of the wages poor. Unless those organizations repent, many will be closed, because their business practices leave much to be desired.

The Bible outlines that some of the workers should be paid on a daily basis, so that they can pay their daily expenses, including food. There are many poor employees going to bed hungry, because of how they are treated by major companies.

The Bible specifically outlines labor laws and how to treat staff. Since the pandemic, there are many who are suffering as a result of the poor treatment they receive from employers.

So, financial literacy is not something that should only be understood by the poor, but the rich too would benefit from financial literacy and the Bible is the blueprint. Many longstanding organizations will be caving in because of their practices. The poor also needs to know that the rich does not keep their money in one place, they have diverse portfolios; including private and commercial real estate and gold, and they also invest in good artwork. They also keep cash on hand in the event of disaster or collapse of the financial market.

Distractions and Missed Opportunities

Nobody wants to experience or even hear the words denial, defeat or delay. We all want to hear positive words like access, approval, success, winning and the list goes on. The greatest hindrance, however, in experiencing success is the word Distraction.

Recognize that distractions come about in many ways.

Technology and Social Network.

Cell phones/iPhones, tablets/iPads, Smart watches, Smart Televisions, Mp3 Players, Video Gaming, Online Dating Services, social media have all become permanent staples in our social lives to the point of addiction and many today can't seem to do without any if not all of these. Most pastors and politicians are closer to their cell phones than to their wives or children or to God. It would be interesting to know of the men and women of God when was the last time they seriously went into the Presence of God, because only in God's Presence will any of us get the necessary solutions we seek. Everything that we need can only be found in the

Presence of God. Matthew 6: 33 reminds us of this. So the very thing that was developed to assist us has now become gods to many of us.

Many companies, especially media organizations, when they are losing market share because of online competitors, they assume that it is as a result of content presentation or what they believe is a lack-luster online marketing strategy. But if they would just put down their cell phones and tablets for a week and get in the presence of God and get new inspiration and ideas from the Source as did the businesspeople of the past, they may very well be amazed at the abundance of ideas they would have. They need to call a retreat – no cell phones, no tablets, in fact, no technology – they would be positively surprised at the results.

Likewise, if the Church Leaders and Politicians started seeking God again without the distraction of mainstream media (CNN, FOX etc), Wall Street's Stock Market analyses, or even of the exchange rates and sliding dollars, then they would be able to see more clearly, the bigger picture of what is ahead and how to capitalize on such things. he cell phones and tablets are not even holy instruments – they were not consecrated for a purpose. So, if you choose to read the Scriptures on those devices in lieu of the holy and inspired Book containing the Word of God, what stops the pop-ups that remind you to buy sex somewhere, or tell you it's okay to masturbate. What stops the phone calls from coming in or the Social Media from sending you reminders? What stops the distractions and allows you to enter the Presence of God to get strategies you need to overcome your daily battles and achieve success.

People

There is a great deal of "noise" in our society today, and it influences what and how we listen and read. These distractions can also lead to deception. When promotions or opportunities come, people can lead you away from it without your realizing it until it's too late. Recognize that when God wants to promote you, He sends/allows people to facilitate it. When the devil wants to stop that promotion, he sends people to distract you. Delilah was Samson's distraction, and it took away his strength, discernment and joy and caused him to make wrong choices and be defeated. Oftentimes, when people don't want you to see, know or understand what is going on (or what they are doing), the "create" the noise – the distraction to shift your focus so that you cannot see the bigger picture. Political strategists, for example, are now getting whipped because they became distracted by their opponents' ploys and were focused on the weaknesses they saw in their opponents, meanwhile those opponents had their own strategies behind the scenes and so these political strategists missed the mark. They did not discern the difference between the battle and the war. Ask any military strategist, you may lose some battles, but you cannot afford to lose the war. Some people get excited about mid-terms, but fail to watch for the "end of term".

Even sports persons get distracted and lose the race when it counts most.

Attacks From Marine Spirits

Symptoms

Dreams that you are:

Swimming in water, naked, eating, are with a past boyfriend / girlfriend / husband / wife; past bosses, old schools and so on.

For Women:
Heavy bleeding, inconsistent periods and cycles, fatigue especially at time of intimacy, attacks after intimacy, miscarriage, problems having children,

For Men:
Dreams of past relationships, premature ejaculation, prostate problems, back pains, dreams of dead relatives and familiar spirits

Explanation:

Marine spirits use incubus and succubus to attack as well as spirit wives and spirit husbands and that is way oftentimes people under this attack will constantly get dreams about oceans and lakes, mermaids. These are the spirits that often attack your marriage, your finance and your health. It causes you to go through great struggles. It causes you to have low self-esteem. Each person must get aggressive with the prayer points to stop the attacks. Never forget the woman with the issue of blood. She lost everything and no doctor could help her; but Jesus touched her. (Mark 5: 25 – 34)

The marine spirits also attack the single women and hinder them from getting married. When you are married, it attacks your spouse.

Prayer Against Marine Spirits

Father, in the name of Jesus Christ of Nazareth, I bind all works of Satan attacking me, attacking my marriage including my sex life, my health including the afflictions and infirmities.

Lord, dry up every heavy bleeding, discharge, pain, urinary flow, my womb/prostate and heal every low blood flow and rectify every premature ejaculation issue. I bind the spirit of Ahab, Jezebel, strife, evil spoken words, every evil altar against me, every family spirit and cut every un-Godly soul ties from past relationships. Destroy by the fire of the Holy Ghost every evil altar against my marriage and from the evil altar that prevents marriage. Destroy the altars that bring frustration to my life. Burn out every cist and every fibroid, enlarged prostate, and be healed now in Jesus' name. Anything that comes against my Body, Sexual Health and Reproductive System.

Father, I ask you to break all marriage covenants with those spirits in Jesus' name. Break and make null and void all spiritual marriage contract agreements with Satan. Make null and void all contracts and agreements with spirit wives and spirit husbands. Divorce and destroy and cut all ties and send them to dry places. Destroy all yokes and bondage, and any garments, wedding rings that are represented in the realm of the spirit – destroy them by the fire of the Holy Spirit

According to Job 41 and Psalm 74 dry up all waters of Leviathan. Put hooks in his mouth. I call the fire of the

Holy Spirit upon his water. I use the blood of Jesus to destroy lust, perversion, generational curses, pride, rejection, evil altar, every anti-prosperity spirit working against my family, my health, my marriage and my finance, through all other spirit wives and spirit husbands and all other marine spirits.

Christ has redeemed me from the curse of the Law and so, I am blessed, my family is blessed, my house is blessed and whatever I touch is blessed.

Chapter 4

PREPARING FOR MARRIAGE

Marriage is a solemn covenant entered into by one man and one woman in perfect freedom, wherein they pledge their love and fidelity in joy, sorrow, sickness, health, prosperity. Marriage is never for the short term. Only God has the power to sever a covenant.

If anyone is planning to get married, he or she must go through the preparation process first. Each must also know the principles and protocols surrounding marriage. There are many with fairy tale versions of what they believe marriage should be.

Is Marriage For You

Recognize that everything you do before you are married impacts the process involved in marriage.

The first and last thing to know is that if you are not willing to yield to God's choice for you to marry, then you are not ready for marriage. (Some are still waiting because they are still holding on to the fairytales in their mind.)

When getting married, you will need to marry a like-minded person. In other words, you must have the same vision and goals.

In marriage, you must be equally yoked not unequally yoked. Either you are both saved or not; but where one is saved and one is unsaved, that marriage is heading for disaster. It is not about the age and the race, but a person's beliefs and faith are key. If both are not the same, you are headed for great pain.

Ensure that in preparation, both know and understand each other's role in the marriage.

Good communication is of utmost importance.

There MUST be leaving and cleaving.
Know that the power of Prayer cannot be understated. It will be one of the greatest tools each person will need in their marriage toolbox.

Each must know the rules that govern sex. Sexual intimacy in a marriage is a privilege and a mystery. Man and wife need each other in this way, because the tensions of life are relieved in this way. If you don't want sex then marriage is not for you.

If you don't want children, marriage is not for you. If you don't want your figure to change in the least, marriage is not for you.

Parental Approval

A part of the preparation for marriage is approval from your parents or your spiritual leader. Once there is confirmation, then it is time to get into premarital counseling. In premarital counseling, the date is set. It should not be a very distant future date, because it opens the door for the couple to fall into temptation and establish un-Godly covenants and soul ties.

Before the Union

Women, ensure that you, like Esther, go through a time of consecration and purification. God wants to purge you from the past, because you cannot afford to take your past into your union – whether or not you had children prior to the union.

Ensure that you have a strong spiritual foundation. Because if you don't have a strong relationship with God, you are not going to have a strong relationship at all.

After the Union

If you are not willing to make sacrifices to birth others - which would sometimes include a delay in your personal goals, then you will have serious problems.
If, as a woman, you are unwilling to yield and allow the man to be the head of the family and help him to maintain that, then there will be problems.

In a marriage, neither of you should be living as if you're still single. Leaving and cleaving means your roles, functions and priorities change significantly.

If, as a man, you are not willing to play your role, which includes feeding his family physically and spiritually, be the father of all the children, nurture and protect his wife and children, just as Christ did with the Church, maintain a strong Spiritual foundation, then you are not ready.

Likewise, the wife needs to pray for her family, and be the Proverbs 31 woman.

Oftentimes people blame God, for the delay, when it is really them unwilling to renew their minds and obey His instructions.

Never go into a marriage covenant thinking about divorce and failure. Enter it confidently and willing to pay the price for a successful marriage.

God hates divorce.

The increase in breakups fuels the increase in crime, violence, economic problems and other social issues.

Stable marriages bring a stable society.

Marriage Is A Gift Not An Office

Many times, people look at marriage as an office. You may be familiar with people talking about the "office of a First Lady" for example. We must understand that an office is temporary and depending on the type of office, people can be voted in or assigned. A gift is something given by God according to His grace. Gifts are permanent; and office is temporary.

The Greek word *"charis"* means *"Grace"*. It does not matter if a person fasts and prays, only God can give that gift whenever He sees it fit. Genesis 2: 23 says, ""This *is* now bone of my bones and flesh of my flesh; She shall be called Woman, because she was taken out of Man."

Based on this Scripture, your gift reflects you, and when one begins to see marriage as a gift and not an office then positive change will begin to take place. Every gift of value must be treated as such – valuable because divine grace and favor comes with it. (Proverbs 18: 22). Normally people give gifts to express love and gratitude and that is exactly what God does to us when a marriage takes place.

There are no material things – a home, cars, gold, silver, jets, boats, nor money more valuable than this gift; and that is why people must be grateful and thankful to the Giver of the gift and treat the gift with respect. Remember Matthew 7: 6.

If a person does not understand the gift, then they need to speak with the gift-giver, because the Gift-Giver has the manual – either the Bible (the Word of God) or the Holy Spirit of God. If you treat the gift poorly then the benefits which come with the gift will go away.

Remember, the gifts do not lose value in times of recession. Many will buy gold and stockpile it all during a recession. However, they ignore the Divine treasure that God has given to sustain them during times of recession. So, a good marriage will stand during the times of recession.

Your spouse is a precious and rare treasure which also comes with many other gifts; and this is why people must thank God each day for the gifts. Hebrews 13: 4 says, *"Marriage is honorable among all, and the bed undefiled; but fornicators and adulterers God will judge."*

"Undefiled" means, *"pure, not made corrupt, not made impure nor unclean"* So when a person goes beyond the boundaries set by God, they will defile their marriage. For example, orgies, bestiality, pedophilia, engaging with robots or a third party, will defile them and cause problems.

God ordained marriage also as a gift to guard against sexual immorality. Married couples must preserve their intimacy from the practices of the world. 1 Corinthians 13: 4 – 7 reminds us that love and patience must be a part of marriage.

1 Peter 3: 7 reminds us that men ought to give honor to the wife, as to the weaker vessel. Not doing so can cause

prayers to be hindered. Likewise, if the woman is not showing respect to her, it can cause similar problems. (Ephesians 5) "Respect" simply means, "to esteem, regard; a feeling of great admiration."

It is critical that every Christian remembers the following scriptures:

Matthew 19: 4 – 6	-	One Flesh
Colossians 3: 18 – 19	-	Submission
1 Peter 4: 8	-	Love Covers A multitude of sins
Proverbs 31: 10	-	Virtue
Proverbs 12: 4	-	Wife Crown of Her Husband

Marriage Is Your Greatest Investment

Your marriage is your greatest investment and is also your biggest asset; greater than stocks and bonds. You have the ability to ensure that there is no depreciation nor loss of value taking place in any way. If most people within our society, particularly the executives would treat their marriage the way they treat other kinds of investments, we would have a better society, because each time such an investment goes down it affects the entire nation and even has impact on crime and violence. The Bible says, if a man cannot rule his own house well, how will he manage the house of God. Managing your household well also impacts every other aspect of the nation's operations. Marriage must also be the number one (1) criteria for selecting people for office. People need to know their lifestyle, since our lifestyles have an impact on our ultimate success.

There are those who have a wife or husband on one hand and the girlfriend or boyfriend on the other hand without realizing that these things have a negative impact on the area of management.

Leave The Baggage Behind

One of the main problems affecting marriages is the baggage brought to the marriage. It is easy to blame the other party while we refuse to deal with the baggage within their lives. The hurt, betrayal, soul ties and failures – we tend to bring them all into the present marriage relationship and begin to blame the present relationship for the shortfalls. We are bringing our past into our future and that is why it hinders us from having a good future. It makes no sense to punish the present relationship for the things/issues of the past in which they had no part. It is unfair to accuse and mistreat your husband or wife today for the problems you had in the past.

Communication Key

This is the key to a successful marriage. However, one thing I have realized with communication is that there cannot be good communication without God. Communication goes beyond academic qualifications; because understanding a person is not about who is more intelligent, it is Spiritual. So, if one is very low spiritually and the other is at a higher level spiritually speaking then here will be problems. It now becomes an issue of being unequally yoked. A cow and a donkey don't usually work well together because their focus and their goals are different so they will be going in two different directions. It is much the same as a Christian being married to a Rastafarian, or an unsaved person, or to someone who believes that the universe is God. At this point, there will be many problems. One may also want to do immoral things as their priority when a Christian cannot do such things.

Sex

Sex is very important. While most are afraid to discuss that topic, and experiences frustrations and attacks they go through to try and enjoy this area, we should not be ignorant to the various laws being passed to come against these benefits and blessings that come with this beautiful gift from God.

Many suffer fatigue/tiredness, issues with their reproductive system and genitals, issues in male health, women's health, and many are paying millions to lure others into sexually immoral activities including masturbation, in addition to the various sites, social networks, sexting, media and music designed to entice the recipient. These things are causing chaos globally. Many are getting into serious legal problems because they are falling morally. It is critical for husbands and wives to ensure they do not withhold from or deny their partners of sex. One of the pillars for a good marriage is a stable sex life which brings happiness and joy, because we were created in such a way that this God-given gift of sex allows us to relieve the tensions and stresses of life, bring joy to the marriage and keep us healthy and balanced.

Remember that in order to have a successful marriage, the bond between husband and wife must be stronger than the parent-child bond. Furthermore, the married couple must be closer to each other than they are to their parents.

Marriage is an incredible investment for anyone willing to enjoy this blessing. Invest in your marriage.

10 Commandments For A Happy Family

(Matthew 6: 33; Proverbs 31; Proverbs 18: 21; Ephesians 4: 26)

1. Seek God First especially when making financial, family and other major decisions!

2. Maintain unity within your household and have one vision for the family. Never compete with but complement each other.

3. Come together, even 1 day each week – for family devotions, giving God thanks for the things He has done for you – both small and big things. Thanksgiving is one of the keys to prosperity and it opens the doors of opportunity for you.

4. Spend family time together! Your family is your biggest investment. More valuable than your house, your vehicle or any other asset. Don't forget the

parks, the movies, the beaches and other family oriented areas and activities.

5. Ensure that you don't allow any third-party intrusion into your family. Communication is key for a healthy family. If communication breaks down, seek Divine, Spiritual help! Never let the sun go down without resolving the issues that are affecting your communication.

6. Declare blessings upon and speak positively about each other. Words are powerful and positive words cancel out the curses that come at you from the enemy daily.

7. Build your family relationships on trust! Avoid speaking negatively against each other or hiding financial Transactions from each other (like secret accounts and so on).

8. Husbands and Wives, pray and ask God to keep your love life vibrant and that you both will satisfy each other.

9. Husbands and Wives, never deny each other of intimacy.

10. Eat healthy foods and exercise regularly.

Things Married Couples Need To Know

✓ It is necessary for you to establish a Prayer Altar in your place of abode – your home.

- ✓ Ensure that you both have one vision.

- ✓ Wives must understand that her first ministry is to her husband.

- ✓ Never be comfortable to the extent that you take things for granted.

- ✓ Wives, understand that she should not allow anything to take precedence over the needs of her husband.

- ✓ A wife needs to submit to her husband and ensure that she is the helper; the help meet for him – to help him in every way to accomplish the will of God.

- ✓ Wives must avoid the Spirit of Familiarity and ensure that she functions in the right spirit and with the right heart.

- ✓ The true success of a woman also comes by way of their husband's success. Oftentimes women who are on a journey toward success, neglect their wifely duties in pursuit of their goals, and that leads to problems. Wives are ministers and wifely duties are not limited to sex. They also include ministering to the emotional, mental, spiritual, and physical needs of their husbands. It also means that she will need to function as his secretary, administrator, financial officer and advisor, and in many other capacities as situations evolve. She wears many hats so that together they can accomplish God's will.

- ✓ Wives must ensure that she avoids any form of rebellion – secret rebellions of the heart. Even if Queen Vashti had gone to the king when he called, her heart would still be saying "NO!"

If Adam had properly instructed Eve on the will and instructions of God for them, and had not been afraid to offend her, then the devil would not have had a foothold in their relationship with God and with each other. The devil was also entertained by her ears and so, wives must also listen to the Holy Spirit who will always speak the truth. She must read the written Word of God and avoid the audio as far as possible. Research also shows that reading the Word is far better for the brain than listening. Any other voice wives listen to beyond their husbands and the Holy Spirit where that voice speaks negatively concerning their marriage, is trespassing in their relationship.

The key to success is your daily activity. A woman cannot be a wife to a man unless she is anointed for this. A man cannot be a husband to a woman unless he is anointed for it. There are many people who want to see themselves as the spouse of an individual without having the grace or anointing for it, or without going through the necessary processing to get there.

When a woman agrees to marry a man, she must understand that she comes under his authority. He is the head of te family. Hence, she needs to understand what he wants, not the other way around. When you are serving, you must know what the person around you needs or wants.

Simple things which make the husband happy.

- ✓ Food and good drinks
- ✓ A Praying Wife (Proverbs 31: 23 - 27)
- ✓ A woman with a gentle spirit [not a quarrelsome woman] (Proverbs 15: 30)
- ✓ A woman with a joyful heart (Proverbs 17: 22)
- ✓ A motivator for their husband
- ✓ A woman who allows a man to be the man as God intended
- ✓ Honor and respect his needs and his vision.
- ✓ An occasional facial and massages

Simple things which make the wife happy:

Gifts, clothes, cologne, jewelry, food
Tell her you love her (flushing out the negative voices)
Decree and declare positive words over her daily.
Encourage and assist her to do the things she would like to accomplish.
Make her your priority by investing in her.
Pray for her.
Be sensitive to her needs.

Be Sensitive To Your Spouse's Needs

- ✓ A man will never have proper success without a virtuous woman.
- ✓ The woman God gives you as a man will birth out of you what God put in you.

- ✓ Remember that men and women are "wired" differently; but God's grace allows you to be one.
- ✓ Always remember that disagreement does not mean it is rebellion.
- ✓ The man must go deeper in order to understand women. He must remember that when God was creating Woman, he was asleep.
- ✓ If a man is not in position, then his family is not in position either.
- ✓ The woman is the other side of the man.

Factors Affecting Marriages

Mark 10: 9 reminds us, *"Therefore what God has joined together, let not man separate."*

There is a great effort globally, from high places, to destroy marriages as we know it. Many of the articles on marriage and divorce which you may read these days, have an air of arrogant vehemence against marriage and seem to celebrate divorce and the negating of the institution of marriage.

Furthermore, the following negatively affects marriages:

- ✓ Disrespect
- ✓ Soul ties
- ✓ Lack of Finance
- ✓ Abundance of Finance
- ✓ Family Lineage (Wrong Family Lineage)
- ✓ Past Hurts
- ✓ Selfishness
- ✓ Pride (Arrogance)

- ✓ Negative words and thoughts of Friends and Family Members

The Wrong Family Lineage

It is important to marry into the correct lineage – that is – the lineage God has specified for you. Many believe that getting married to someone they love or like, or to someone with money, is the green light for marriage. However, God has a deeper spiritual plan for you to marry into the right lineage as that determines your spiritual inheritance.

God takes lineage very seriously and we must allow Him to choose for us. Being in the right lineage affects the following:

- ✓ Wealth Transfer
- ✓ Spiritual Inheritance
- ✓ Purpose and Calling

Some lineages have been deeply tainted so that the people no longer believe in God or have delved very deeply into witchcraft. Furthermore, there are those who are automatically an enemy to your purpose and calling and has to potential to corrupt the bloodline if children are born of that union.

Being married to the wrong person also means that you are unequally yoked. Being unequally yoked brings pain. (For example, while you may want to go to church service, they want to go parties.

No one wants to know that they have married into the lineage of Jezebel and Ahab.

The devil knows the great sacrifice a righteous family makes, especially with prosperity and wealth so he will send someone to corrupt the family line in order to destroy the hard work and Godly inheritance. Remember how insistent Abraham was for his servant to go and find the right wife for Isaac. Abraham knew that if Isaac married the wrong woman, His entire wealth and hard work would go to naught. We see it also in the book of Nehemiah where the Lord instructed that His people put away their pagan wives.

The truth is, Satan hates a Godly marriage, because it brings blessings and is a covenant with God. When a covenant is broken, as the book of Malachi says, there are consequences and rewards.

The right lineage and being equally yoked are 2 important factors in a strong marriage. Compatibility in this instance is inevitable because the two would share the same God, Vision, Principles, Values, and general way of thinking. As such it opens the door for a healthy and wholesome marriage relationship between husband and wife.

Remember always, that marriage also impacts governments, economies and nations and influences crime, violence, and the moral fabric of any society, so even more so, GOD HATES DIVORCE!

Many Reasons For Divorce

In order to deal with divorce, we need to first understand why the marriages are breaking up. We also need to understand Spiritual Warfare.

There are many in the Kingdom of darkness who are assigned specifically to fight to destroy marriages and take down families, and if you are not willing to fight, then you will be added to the statistics. (Ephesians 6).

The Gender Agenda has been put in place to create a new family dynamic and norm; and that new dynamic does not carry the blessing of God. Remember, God created one man for one woman with specific instructions. (Genesis 1: 27 – 28). As such, divorce will terminate that instruction, which in turn affects the population, hinders Godly offspring, and sets the trajectory for the elimination of man's dominion and purpose.

Divorce also strengthens Satan's plans in a nation (John 10: 10). It opens the door for adultery, fornication, same-sex relationships and is in fact the opposite of God's instruction to man to be fruitful and multiply. (Genesis 1: 28).

What Divorce Brings To The Table

Divorce brings:

Division
Distraction
Defeat

Death
Delay
Deception
Destruction
Decline in Morals
No country can be great when divorce becomes the order of the day.

The Benefits of Marriage

Marriage brings increase when it is done according to God's design. Recognize that part of God's design is that we marry the right person, that is, the person He selects for us. Marriage brings:

- ✓ Godly Offspring
- ✓ Land ownership and possession
- ✓ Cash and Assets
- ✓ Various types of wealth
- ✓ Spiritual strengthening

Marriage also affords us God-centered unity, coupled with the Power of Agreement to decree, declare and establish God's covenant on earth as the union worships Him as one. This relationship of marriage is also symbolic of the Church; and so, divorce affects the Church in a significant way.

Always remember this: There are some things that can only be released to us by God when we enter into the covenant of marriage.

The "Beneficiaries" of a Broken Covenant

- ✓ The State
- ✓ Lawyers
- ✓ The Health Industry
- ✓ Mental Health Institutions
- ✓ Financial Institutions
- ✓ Media
- ✓ The Gender Agenda

What We Need To Know

a) If you don't know or understand your role in a marriage – whether you are male or female, don't marry yet.

b) Know the value of marriage. Marriage is more important and more significant than your title, job, or money.

c) A person's relationship with God is a reflection of their relationship in marriage.

d) It is extremely important to the health of your marriage to build on God's foundation. If the woman is not the missing rib of the man to whom she is married, **Trouble**! If the man has taken on the wrong rib – **Trouble!**

e) God's blessing does not rest on unequal yoking.

f) Making choices for marriage Hollywood-style – that is, based on looks, finance, emotions, and connections, is in true "Young and the Restless, Days of Our Lives" fashion and is not what God said.

g) Women, please stop the hunting and seeking and let the man fulfill his role. (Proverbs 18: 22)

h) Good Communication and Prayer a big part of the covenant.

i) Understand truly what it is to leave and cleave. Your past baggage must go as there are things you will need to let go from the past in order to grow and move forward in the union.

j) Both parties need to understand what submission truly means and that it first begins with submission to God.

k) Avoid denying each other the benefits of your union. If you believe in denying your spouse of sex, then don't get married. It was never meant to be a tool for manipulating your spouse.

Fight For Your Marriage

Remember that the first man and woman were a microcosm (a small-scale version) of the Church. Marriage was created to bring glory to God.

There are many battles we have in life, however, this battle for Marriage God's way, is one of the most important battles. It is time to destroy the current statistics.

Maintaining Your Marriage Vows

Marriages are under attack and even nations are putting laws in place that are anti-marriage or are amending laws to dissolve marriages quickly.

Many don't know that when vows are broken it brings serious negative impact on the economy, security, crime levels and the nation in general. The establishment of marriage vows carries with it benefits such as favor, grace, access and all that is a great blessing. God takes marriage vows very seriously and Malachi 2: 16 says: *"For the Lord God of Israel says That He hates divorce, for it covers one's garment with violence," Says the Lord of hosts. "Therefore, take heed to your spirit, that you do not deal treacherously."*

Furthermore, Matthew 19: 6 says, *"So then, they are no longer two but one flesh. Therefore, what God has joined together, let not man separate."*

There are so many things that are rising to break marriage vows and separate husbands and wives – laws, policies, regulations, sexual immorality. There are many websites that have been set up to bring down many morally and spiritually. There are many websites where people can purchase sexual services. There are robots that have been created to for the sole purpose of a man or woman's sexual satisfaction – all of which are immoral. Open marriages are now the order of the day for many worldwide.

When divorce takes place, it eats away at the fabric of society. Some people may believe that when divorce takes place then you can jump into another relationship and then all is well. Similar to the Hollywood happenings.
Every covenant carries four (4) factors/elements – Parties (those directly involved), Conditions, Results and Security; and when these elements are not satisfied and the covenants are broken, there are serious consequences. Every person involved must ensure that their vows/covenant remain intact.

Communication

Every person involved in a contract, especially in marriage, must communicate with each other, and do so in such a way that everyone understands what is being communicated. Grace, love and respect are extremely important. Most marriages start to decline as misunderstandings take place. Recognize that every time you try to pass the blame on to the other person, God is pointing His finger at you too.

In communication, mannerisms are very important. That is why it is critical for us to get to know the other person by seeking God first who will reveal truths. Each party must make every effort to understand his/her role. Understand that there is no marriage that will not have some kind of communication issue. Cultures, spiritual growth /development, mindsets all differ, so there may not be an immediate meeting of the minds, but growth takes time; and remember, change is not one-sided it requires both sides.

Fight For Your Union Not Against It

Sexual Purity is key to good governance, regardless of profession – politics, church – so when a person is not walking in sexual purity it affects every aspect of society, even the Justice System, and lends itself to inequality in distribution. There are many in society trying to get their drive and zeal in the wrong way – threesomes, orgies, children, animals and toys. Meanwhile, by so doing, they have breached the contract and that carries consequences.

The greatest threat to climate change is the breaking of marriage vows. Even in politics, I wouldn't encourage husbands and wives to go into representational politics together. Where one enters representational politics, the other needs to maintain stability at home so that the family unit remains protected. When a politician's life is not in order, it also impacts the people they represent. It is not even advised to have bodyguards of the opposite gender to watch over your spouse because this can lead to infidelity. There needs to be balance. Spending long periods away from your spouse is also something that each would need to look into; distance for long periods is not a healthy practice for any marriage covenant.

Without a healthy family there cannot be a healthy society, and for people to have and maintain true prosperity and their inheritance, it is critical for them to fight to uphold their marriage vows.

Marriage Over Money

The Book of Malachi is a good book to read particularly for families. It outlines God's unchanging love for His people, as well as rebuke and exhortation. He also addresses, in no uncertain terms, the treachery of priests and laymen divorcing faithful wives and marrying heathen women who are idolaters. This is followed by a plea for them to guard their passions and to be faithful to the wife of their youth who was given to them by the Lord.

We have seen for ourselves that the divorce rate is skyrocketing and this is so even and especially among Christians. Oftentimes, the central culprit for the divorce is money. Even nations are now falling apart because they have prioritized money over family. When the security budgets and the anti-Christ agenda have been put to the fore, ahead of marriage and family – it is clear to see that the nations are in trouble.

Psalm 89: 14 says, *"Righteousness and justice are the foundation of Your throne; Mercy and truth go before Your face."*

This is the pillar of every nation and family. This is why we must pray for righteous leader who fully support the family and know well the importance of building and supporting strong families.

Focus On These Things

Avoid comparisons. Many times, a person will look down on their spouse and only focus on their shortcomings. They may not have money, but they display time and love, which leads to a healthy marriage. There are many with a lot of money, but they don't spend a lot of time with their spouse and family. Unity and respect are the keys to a successful marriage.

Malachi 2: 16 says, *"For the Lord God of Israel says That He hates divorce, for it covers one's garment with violence," says the Lord of hosts. "Therefore, take heed to your spirit, That you do not deal treacherously."*

God And Covenants

God is serious about covenants. When two people marry, God stands as a witness to the union. Covenants speak of faithfulness and enduring commitment. Divorce is a violent act to God's intention.

When a covenant is broken, it brings judgment and penalties to the family and to everything to which it is connected. When God wants to do something, he makes a covenant. (Genesis 6). That is why God could protect Noah. The Ark was protected by a covenant with God. The giving of a token – the ring – is a sign to seal the covenant. (Genesis 9: 9 – 11).

There is also:

Covenant between God and the earth, as well as God and man – hence the Rainbow. (Genesis 9: 8 – 17).

Biblical covenant, including the covenant sacrifice with the shedding of blood, covenant meals (Genesis 8: 20)

We also see a final establishment of covenant in Genesis 9: 9 & 13.

Further to this, God cannot make a covenant with anything that is not clean, and this is the reason we see such detail in His instructions about giving burnt offerings.

All this being said, everything must be done to maintain your covenant. When a covenant is broken it is very serious.

No Competition

Married Spouses should never compete with each other. Instead, they must complement each other. They should not speak down to each other in the presence of their children, especially where they speak negative words concerning each other. For example, a husband may tell his wife "Leave, you Jezebel!" But in doing so they have released a curse over their wife and themselves as there isn't a Jezebel without an Ahab. So, kind words are key!
The man is not a woman, and the woman is not a man; and as such one does not function like the other. Many women have a lot of issues like the spirit of rejection, fear and the experience of verbal abuse. The man must be more patient toward his wife; and whenever arguments arise, they must stop and pray.

Husbands and wives must walk in unity with each other – having the same financial goals, spend wisely, where it applies, they need to file their taxes together, ensure that they take care of the child/children who are outside of the marriage. They must not hide financial secrets from each other. All these can significantly affect the marriage.

Always remember that one's marriage is important and do everything to protect it. Seek counseling where necessary. Spend time with the family and treasure every moment you spend together.

Value Your Marriage

A higher percentage of marriages are crumbling today, and some that look good on the outside are unstable within. Some are just for show to appease others and the children - and the issues that cause them to crumble are simple things like credit cards, bills, closet space, long working hours, and the 3rd-party influence (friends or family).

Never make decisions in your household based on the opinions of others. So, what if your friends buy new homes, vehicles or gets opportunities that you don't.

Some of you are taking advice from people whose marriages have failed, or who have never been married.

There are even people, who will starve their partners of time and sex by becoming occupied with other things, getting degree after degree, while their marriage is crumbling. They do it to compete. Remember, every marriage comes with a covenant and breaking these covenants carries serious consequences.

Always marry who God says for love and for fulfillment of purpose. Any other motives will bring pain and headaches. Remember that there are gold-diggers and opportunists out there on both sides. There are also very good actors around but when the costumes are removed, that is when you will see the true character. Then it will be too late for a refund. Good men and women still exist but you must look beyond what the natural eyes see and trust God for His choice. Marriage is more than sex, more than the wedding ceremony. It is not a "Mills and Boon" Situation, it is real life. There are no roses without thorns. When someone's marriage fails then everything else falls apart. That is the reason it is so valuable. Many times, when marriages fail, people become bitter, but they don't accept that they are not blameless.

Know this! Dating and having sex do not determine whether a person is marriage material or not, because there are actors who can play any role, and after the Opening Night, God help you!

How To Pray For Your Marriage

Prayer is the most important key when fighting for your marriage. The enemy wastes no time in launching attacks at us and at marriages, so we can't waste any time either in countering the attacks.

Therefore, pray the following Prayer Points:

- **Uncommon Unity** – Pray that Uncommon Unity will exist between you both.

- **Discern The Enemies Of Your Marriage** – Pray that you will both discern any Judases, Jezebels or Delilahs in your midst.

- **Soul Ties and Strongholds** – Pray that God will break all Soul-Ties from past relationships will break; and all strongholds.

- **Evil Altars** – That God will destroy every evil altar that has been established to bring down your marriage.

- **Marine Spirits/Marine Witchcraft** – Pray that God will destroy every Marine Spirits working against your marriage and union. In order to know if Marine Spirits are working against your marriage (or if evil altars have been established) pay attention to your dreams. Where you see yourself having intercourse in your dreams or marrying someone when you are already married, that is an indication of the presence of Marine Spirits attacking your union.

- **Sex Life in the Marriage And Health** – Pray that your sex life will be "on fire". Pray also for patience in each of you; as well as good communication between you both. Pray also for physical and emotional healing for each other.

- **Money and A Third-Party** – Pray that neither money, nor a third-party will come between you. That includes relatives and friends.

- **Unity in Prayer** – Pray that there is unity in prayer and that the husband will wash his wife with the Word.

- **One Vision** – Pray that you both will have one vision – one set of goals and directions – so that the family unit can go in one direction according to the Will of God.

➢ **Quality Time** – Spend quality time with each other and ensure that neither withholds sex from each other.

➢ **Increasing Grace** – Pray that God will increase Grace, Mercy, Compassion and Favor each day.

➢ **Singular View** – Pray that God will give the husband eyes only for his wife and that the wife's breasts will satisfy her husband.

Chapter 5

MARRIED PEOPLE SHOULD HAVE MORE SEX

God has given us the gift of sex for procreation, emotional joy and physical fulfillment of sexual union. Sexual union is reserved for married people and must be enjoyed regularly in that union so that couples can also avoid temptation. It must be maintained in wholeness through faithfulness and purity of heart, discipline of the eyes and consecration of the body. (1 Corinthians 7: 3 – 5; Proverbs 5: 15 – 20; Job 31: 1; Genesis 2: 24)

It is critical for Christians to pray more for each married couple to have a healthy sexual life, especially in light of all the attacks that are launched daily against married couples and their sexual lives – including the promotion and sale of artificial penises and vaginas, robots, as well as masturbation and prostitution. This while people are fighting to legislate laws to limit married couples from having regular sex and passing laws for unmarried couples to have more sex.

Let it be clear that marriage is consent for having sex, and it is scriptural. Withholding sex will only bring more divorces, more masturbation and more rape. Ultimately, it will stop Godly offspring from coming forth. It is an attack on the Church and marriages and the enemy is after the mystery of Christ and the Church (Ephesians 5: 32).

The Church has to change its strategy. Instead of fighting within, focus on the spiritual warfare that is taking place against it. We are up against marine spirits that are unleashed on the people, and very shortly, there will be laws to make fornication, adultery and we know to be indecent exposure, legal. In fact, it has already begun.

The book of Solomon clearly shows strategies for married couples regarding sex. Man's deepest need is to experience the oneness of authentic love, in a dependable relationship.

The Songs of Solomon depict a woman as an enclosed, private, protected garden for royal use, into which she invites her beloved to enter. Never withhold sex from your spouse. (Songs 4: 9 & 5: 1) God made the breasts and the lips to satisfy. More kissing is needed between married couples.

Honey, milk, wine are used as a comparison for kissing – and they are all good for the body. Something happens when married couples kiss. It brings healing and deliverance. Most married people no longer kiss. (Songs 7: 7 – 8)

The book also speaks to us about the different fruits and drinks a person should take to add spice to the marriage relationship.

Both husband and wife must speak about life over each other and compliment each other on a regular basis. (Songs 4: 16) Always remember that this is also a Promised Land and a great investment that God has given you.

Many times, married couples experience attacks such as fatigue when they want to engage in sex, and it is time for them to fight back; to break every attack upon their lives.

God wants each and every married couple to enjoy sex so that there is no room for adultery. Adultery allows a person to lose his/her authority. So it is critical to fight for your sex life and have sex regularly.

The book of Solomon also outlines the different perfumes and oils, blended beverages, and the apples and raisins that can be used. Washing each other's feet, a nice massage, manicure and/or pedicure can do wonders. Don't dress at home as if you are at church services. A little purple in the hair and a few hair extensions don't hurt. (Songs 7: 5)

There needs to be openness and good communication to deal with the happenings that are taking place today. The world is supposed to look on and want to be married. So married people can't just sit by while the world is enjoying sex more than they are enjoying. Withholding sex or becoming complacent in your marriage will bring disaster.

Refuse and abstain from any sexual encounters before marriage. Simply put, keep your virginity until the time of marriage and avoid any situations that arouse or awaken sexual desires and activities before marriage. God created sex to be wonderful and fulfilling but only within the boundaries of marriage.

Wives, always declare Songs of Solomon (Songs) 4: 16

"Awake, O north wind, and come, O south! Blow upon my garden that its spices may flow out. Let my beloved come to his garden and eat its pleasant fruits."

Husbands always declare Songs of Solomon (Songs) 4: 9 - 11

"You have ravished my heart, my sister, my spouse; you have ravished my heart with one look of your eyes, with one link of your necklace. How fair is your love, my sister, my spouse! How much better than wine is your love, and the scent of your perfumes than all spices! Your lips, O my spouse, drip as the honeycomb; honey and milk are under your tongue; …"

Masturbation Brings Mind Pollution

Proverbs 16: 2 says, *"All the ways of a man are pure in his own eyes, but the Lord weighs the spirits."*

We are living in a time where many are promoting a society without boundaries which they call a free society. That means you are free to do whatever you want to do with your body, no moral, social values and no limits. We must remember that we are either a slave to sin or a slave to righteousness. In pursuing freedom, many find themselves in bondage.   No one can serve two (2) masters. Masturbation is one such thing that will mess up your mind and your spirit. Our spirit is important. God wants man to be whole – spirit soul and body. (I Thessalonians 5: 23) When your spirit is polluted, you are not able to discern truth from lies and you make wrong choices/poor decisions and things are done in the wrong spirit, and God wants us to have pure hearts and a right spirit. (Psalm 51; Proverbs 20: 27) It is sin that has separated man from God and it destroyed that strong and healthy relationship man had with God. So when your mind is polluted – in the same way that negativity and negative music can pollute one's spirit – it denies you of even your daily benefits and what God has in store for you. God's word says, "…as a man thinks, so is he." So when we sing about things that are opposite to the Word and will of God for our lives, then it manifests accordingly. When we begin to speak or sing about 'dawgs' and engaging in oral sex, or having girls in twos, threes, sevens and elevens – once the mind is polluted, the manifestation is not far behind. The diversion from the natural purpose of what God intended sex to be will bring pollution especially of the mind and spirit. So as a result of some of that, more families are in turmoil and we will also see it playing out among our babies in the schools.

Masturbation and the Transfer of Spirits

There is such a thing as a transference of spirit – good or bad. In the Bible, when God is going to bless people or have an act of ordination, he instructs that hands be laid upon the people to give them power and that those laying hands have and excellent spirit to carry out the function.

What if that leader is masturbating, what will happen? There will be a transfer of an unclean spirit. (Numbers 11: 16 – 17, also Isaiah 42: 5; Zachariah 12: 1) What about the person who does your hair, nails, massages you who may be masturbating? There will be a transfer of an unclean spirit to you, and at some point, you may find yourself doing it too. Your head, feet hands, eyes, mouth and sexual organs are gates of the human body/spirit/soul, and it will open the door to other unclean acts. Most people who are involved in masturbation have restless nights enjoying their sexual relationships with their spouse. It also opens the door for unclean spirits named incubus and succubus that attack them in their dreams and the result is what many know as wet dreams. In the Bible, when people had this issue, God would instruct them to wash. (Leviticus 15: 16 – 17)

People who engage in masturbation will have serious psychological effects which leads to isolation, abuse and competing with their spouses. If a person is single, it takes longer to get to the point of marriage and it would bring serious problems and pain after marriage. Hosea 4: 6 says, "My people are destroyed for lack of knowledge…"

God created sex but there are borders and boundaries (Hebrews 13: 4) our bodies are the temple of God, we don't have ownership, we have stewardship. Spiritually, our hands are very important. They represent power, strength, service, oath of allegiance, honor, and worship of God as well as blessings. It is even critical to know that not everyone should hold your hands nor shake hands with. Spiritually and naturally, diseases can be contracted by

touching hands. Here's a question: Why would someone masturbate when God has given them a wife/husband?
Sex is good, but beyond the context of what God said, it pollutes us and what God designed for us to be a blessing, we by our actions, make it a curse. When people are masturbating, they have to think about other people and so that in itself will pollute your mind especially if you are in a marriage relationship.

The Importance of Sex For Married Couples

Marriages are under attack particularly Christian marriages. Laws are being implemented today that conflict with Christian beliefs. Christians should not be ignorant that the enemy hates Christian marriages.

If, for example, the law is passed regarding marital rape, we will see a spike in crime, violence, abortion and more divorces will be added to the books. Furthermore, the spirit of rejection will run rampant and hate and bitterness will increase. Love between husband and wife will diminish and marriages will simply be about money. Additionally, suicide, masturbation and other immoral activities will also increase. There is a crisis.

There are great attacks on the sex life of many Christians through witchcraft and various issues arising. It is imperative for Christian couples to enjoy sex regularly. (1 Corinthians 7: 3 – 5). Having sex often stops temptation and steers you away from sexual immorality. It also reduces stress. It also causes blessings to flow and brings pleasure, and procreation. (Genesis 1: 27 – 28). If we don't have sex, how will we be able to execute the instruction God first gave to husband and wife.

Sex strengthens the bond and love between husband and wife, and married couples should not allow themselves to become to busy or so involved with the children and other activities that they don't have time or are too tired for each other. Remember, lack of sex can reduce intimacy for each other and allow a third party to enter, and open the door for rejection and resentment. So it is critical for married couples to speak words of blessing and strength over each other and over their sex life.

When marriages fail, it sends a negative message about the Church.

Sex between husband and wife is a good gift given to us by God and should never be withheld.

In The Beginning

Sex was part of God's created order for man. (Genesis 2: 25). Furthermore, they were both naked and were not ashamed; but sin opened the door for all manner of un-Godly, unclean activities and lifestyles against God's created order.

The two biggest areas of attack for marriages are sex and communication. Both male and female suffer greatly in silence and are afraid to speak about that area.

Regardless of all that happens, faithfulness to each other and to God must be maintained. Every man must read Proverbs 5:15-20 for revelation and practice it.

Members of the Body of Christ need to stop ignoring the issue, move past their hang-ups and pray for marriages and the sex life of married couples with fervor – remembering James 5: 16. We can't afford to be shy about the issue of sex, the fight is on and the battle must be fought and won.

Stop! And Start Again

Married couples:

Stop Allowing Social Networks To Steal Quality Time. Do not allow social networks/media to rob you of valuable and quality time with your spouse and your family. Hiding passwords from each other, allowing 'ex-friends/ex-partners' to give you counsel about your marriage, posting pictures of past relationships with other friends commenting, exposes your family to verbal attacks and can have significant and grave consequences for your marriage and family life.

Stop Deliberately Depriving Each Other Of Sex. This is never to be a weapon in your marriage. The Bible is clear on it in I Corinthians 7: 1 – 5 and Ephesians 5: 22 – 24. Sex is a part of the covenant ascribed by God to husband and wife married to each other.

Stop Neglecting The Joys Of An Exciting Sex Life. Change our eating habits and set up a health plan for fitness.

Be careful of personal trainers. Engage in healthy weight management together and embrace the use of natural remedies – herbs, fruits, vegetables and nuts – to help you maintain a healthy and exciting sex life. Get back to basics and enjoy the benefits of these foods that God created, including Melons, Lettuce, Almonds, Unsalted Peanuts, Walnuts, Flax Seeds, Sesame Seeds, and Pumpkin Seeds and invest in a good blender or extractor. Ezekiel 47: 12 reminds us that the leaves bring healing and God wants us healed body, soul and spirit, and at the same time, get a revelation of the benefits of the natural gifts He has given us.

Start Enjoying Each Other Again through this God-given gift called sex.

Pray For A Healthy Sex Life

As the institution of marriage continues to come under attack, in particular within the Christian countries, it is the duty of all Christians to pray for God-given illumination. There is a difference between illumination and inspiration. Illumination refers to the influence of the Holy Spirit which helps Christians to grasp the things of God. (I Corinthians 2: 4; Matthew 16: 17) All Spiritual knowledge must be by revelation.

The Christian marriages are under attack by Canaanite cults. God has given Christians the resource of the Holy Spirit and the Word of God. Christians need to be wary of theologians who want to interpret Scripture without a belief in or acceptance of the Holy Spirit! That is very dangerous! Many people are turning away from Christianity because they are tired of religiosity – they want to see the power of God manifest in their lives!

There are three stages of marriage recorded in the Bible that all Christians should know.

- ➢ Contract (Genesis 29: 15 – 20; Genesis 24: 33,51-54,57-58)
- ➢ Consummation (Genesis 29: 21 – 26; Genesis 24: 64-67)
- ➢ Celebration (Genesis 29: 27 – 28;)

Once one becomes married, it becomes a contract and a consent to have sex. Once the contract is breached - even through withholding sex … I want to hear what the legal minds have to say about that! What happens when a contract is breached? When a contract is breached it becomes voidable. So the party in the right can terminate! Hence, divorce lawyers and the courts will be making a lot of money at the expense of family!

Christian marriages are what is deemed as Covenant Marriages! The Devil hates it because it becomes a 'threefold chord' which is not easily broken. What people should be lobbying for instead is for laws to be put in place to deal with adultery and fornication, and deal with those going beyond the Scriptural boundaries of marriage, and enforce that there be restitution physically and financially to those they have hurt.

An attack on Christian marriages is ultimately and attack on the Church. When married people engage in sex, it is spiritual warfare against the enemy, because what we are in fact doing is reproducing the image of God in which we were made and procreating as He instructed!

Thus:
- You must invest in your Sex Life!

- Anoint both you and your spouse's sexual areas each day and speak life to any mountain! For example, Premature Ejaculation, Mind Attacks During Sex, Low Feeling, Loss of Sexual Desire for you, Losing Interest in Sex, Witchcraft from people who want to break up your marriage!

- Good sex brings healing and joy and lets you relax at work and helps you think clearly, and this not only supports mental health, but is part of prosperity as well.

- Your sex life is the most important part of the marriage. God wants you to enjoy sex – the enemy does not want you to enjoy it in marriage, he instead wants to go after sex in un-Godly relationships and using unnatural devices. The one thing you must understand Sex in marriage give God worship! (NB Sex outside of marriage glorifies the devil.)

- Ask the Lord to cut off all soul ties with past lovers, and free your mind of them and yourself of the feelings! Don't bring the past relationships and issues into the present one!

- Irish Moss, Carrot Juice, Barley, Pumpkin Seed, Soursop and Soursop Leaf are good for both you and your spouse! In addition to the nutritional value, these serve to enhance a person's sex life!

➢ Drink a lot of water before having sex!

➢ Exercise at least twice per week.

➢ Play Romantic Music – particularly the ones you liked when you first met each other!

➢ Try different positions, not just the 'Missionary Position': and try different places too – your swimming pool, the car, the beach – variety is the spice of life!

➢ If you are Spirit-filled, pray in tongues quietly and use the Blood of Jesus, before and during sex that you will have the stamina and drive.

➢ Give each other a massage and help each other relax.

➢ Do not allow the children to interfere with your Sex Life! Send them over to the grandparents for the weekend and go relax at a hotel, or dinner and a movie!

In addition to that, good home-cooked chicken soup and a good warm bath also helps!

Pray the Word of God daily to have a successful marriage and a good sex life! Remember that the enemy is working overtime to destroy covenant marriages!

Chapter 6

GET BACK TO BASICS

There are a number of things happening in our society today which may seem disrespectful, particularly toward society's seniors and the great men and women – icons - of times past. It is critical for us to get back to basics in the home. Everything starts in the home and should be maintained in the school environment. The nation has been compromising in the area of discipline. Some compromise in order to find favor with international bodies and individuals. Further to this, parents ought not to allow the airwaves to be our babysitters and mentors for our children. We have allowed the dress code in the schools and offices to slide downwards.

For anyone invited, there is a specific dress code for Buckingham Palace, and it must be respected and maintained. We have compromised with nudity as a nation because of lust and greed and now we are shame-faced and embarrassed. The disrespect and lack of civic pride shown with regard to someone who helped to bring awareness to the diversity and uniqueness of our nation, and to cause many to embrace the very things that represent our nation, and the warmth, joviality and creativity of our nation is sad.

Simple Manners

Never try to build a legacy by disrespecting others within society. Always walk in humility – pride goes before a fall.

Anything we do should be done for the protection of our children and to uplift others. Many in the media are airing things that expose our children to the wrong things at an early age.

Don't go to the social media pages of others and post disrespectful comments. Even if you don't agree, either keep it in the context of constructive criticism or don't respond or react to it at all.

Whenever you are corrected by your boss, pastor or a senior member of society in general about your attitude and behavior or how to improve yourself, don't talk back and ask them about themselves. Use it as an opportunity to build yourself and grow. If you take the opposite attitude, your tenure will be short-lived wherever you go.

Always learn the protocol of the house/office/church or of the environment wherever you go. Don't go in wanting to change rules at the get go. Observe and learn. Oftentimes people enter into a group, organization or industry to disrupt and change – if you don't agree then find another organization and move on.

Don't go into someone's home and immediately start to "investigate" what they have, how they got it, where they got it from and how you can get one. Don't go into their refrigerator or cut off a piece of their flowers or take of the pot cover to see what they cooked and put your hand in it.

Always close the doors gently so-to-speak when you are leaving an organization. Don't try to speak negatively about the organization, the boss or the co-workers you had there, because at some point you will face it again. You are going to need a recommendation, or they will be called to give an opinion of you.

Simple principles

So, we need to get back to basics. Simple things such as saying 'good morning' or 'good afternoon' to those we pass should resume. Furthermore, always address people by their titles! 'Mr, Mrs, Your honor, sergeant, colonel, president, prime minister, Rev' and so on. Never use the term 'you guys' when addressing your leaders or those above you in a conversation with them.

Always have respect for a person's office (position). You may think they are unworthy of the position, but they are in positions of authority and should you one day be in a position of authority, the treatment you issue will be the same treatment that meets you!

Regardless of the relationship (or lack of one) address your mother and father with respect when speaking to them - especially if you desire to have long life!
Say please, excuse me, and thank you. Don't enter a person's office, home or room without being invited to do so.

Don't take a seat unless invited to do so.

Men: Don't pray or eat with your head covered; once you enter a building remove your hat (or headgear) as a sign of reverence/respect.

Women: When you are in an interview, dress appropriately (nothing too tight, too short or too long). Sit with your legs together.

Men: Unless otherwise instructed, dress professionally for interviews.
Don't engage in phone conversations during church services or any other formal functions/gatherings; excuse yourself and step outside.

No gum chewing while you talk.

Young People: When in public (transportation or buildings) always offer a seat to elders, pregnant women and those with disabilities.

God Has A Dress Code Too

One of the most serious declines that have taken place over the years on a global level is the decline in the dress code.

Many parents have failed badly in this area, because learning how to dress oneself is a skill that is learned at home.

Set The Standard

The older women ought to be teaching the younger women, but that is sorely lacking in our society today. Fathers are supposed to take a stand. The government should also maintain strict dress code policies within the government offices. Church leaders should no longer compromise for the sake the offering or growth.

God has a standard. I am not talking about pants versus skirts or the mixing of materials. I am talking about the way we carry ourselves today, and the lack of regard, not just for self, but for the House of God, government offices, institutions of learning and so on.

Have you ever stopped to realize that everything that is considered precious is always covered? In fact, according to the Bible, anything that was uncovered was considered unclean. So everything in the temple has to be covered, and we are the temple of the Living God, so we need to be covered. Recognize that external adornment does not determine one's beauty. True beauty is internal.

No Hypocrisy

While many legislate for laws regarding sexual harassment in the workplace, there are those who cover even less of themselves in the workplace or are wearing their clothes even tighter to encourage sexual encounters or as a means of manipulation and control. There are people within society today who feel that they should dress in any way they please, wearing whatever they please wherever they please. For example, wearing a sleeveless shirt or dress in government offices or classrooms or on television, yet if they must stand before a judge in a court of law, they wear a suit or robe. Both Police and Military have different attire for different functions, and they **must** adhere to it.

If you were invited to Buckingham Palace to Prince Harry and Meghan's Wedding, you would be required by the Queen and the Archbishop of Canterbury to adhere to a particular dress code which would include a hat and a skirt suit/jacket with sleeves (for women), a tuxedo (for men) or a specific military uniform (for those who serve). Failure to adhere to those requirements would mean your being removed from the premises. So even Beyonce, Lady Gaga and Ishawna would have to comply, and do so without complaint.

Church

In the Bible, the Lord would instruct the priests to dress in a particular way, and that had nothing to do with being religious. (an excuse used by many today) Nowadays, our worship leaders and even some church leaders, come to church in ripped jeans with their skin (and more) in public view. Some come to church in clothing so tight that it leaves nothing to the imagination, and no one can focus. Where are the respect and honor for God? Every person should read Malachi 1: 6 – 8. We have respect for the politicians and secular leaders, but have none for God, nor His House, nor His people. People even want to wear shorts to church services. There is no way that should be allowed by any Pastor who understands how to truly honor God.

Many on social media would cheer on the moral decline calling them bold, modern moves. And some of these activists who cheer others on, when they go to certain countries, they must cover up from head to toe with only their eyes visible and they gladly do it!

When people are too "free" they eventually lose their freedom. Every organization has a right to determine what type of dress code fits their environment and it must be respected whether it is religious or secular.

Moral decline is what wrecks a nation, organization and the economy. We need to take a stand, particularly with our children.

Moral And Spiritual Breakdown

The most dangerous things that can happen to a nation are moral and spiritual collapse.

Our nation has been heading in this direction for a long time and now it seems to have accelerated toward this dangerous place. No doctor can effectively treat any illness or issue unless they have properly diagnosed the patient. Thereafter, they can begin to apply correct remedy to ensure restoration of good health.

Foundational Cracks

There are many within society today who are ignoring the obvious moral and spiritual breakdown taking place at every turn. Some believe that building roads and other tangible infrastructure, and the implementation of Artificial Intelligence (AI) throughout the entire societal framework, and the subtle mandating of vaccination will bring change to the society. However, when there is moral and spiritual breakdown, it means that the foundation is cracked and any builder will tell you that when the foundation cracks, no matter what you build on it, it is just a matter of time before everything comes falling.

Leadership

Moral and spiritual breakdown starts from the top. When this happens, particularly in a Christian-based, God-centered society, the first "plan of action" given is always to secularize the society by rejecting God and the principles of God, pushing the Church into a corner – showing no respect to the Church by deeming it irrelevant, while promoting money and carnal, immoral activities as relevant to economic growth which is then deemed as the savior of the nation.

Identifying Moral and Spiritual Breakdown

Here a some of the things we will see when there is moral and spiritual breakdown in a society.

- ✓ Disorder
- ✓ Lack of Value for Life
- ✓ Significant increase in levels of Crime and Violence
- ✓ Exploitation and Disappearance of Children
- ✓ Significant increase in rape
- ✓ Less marriages taking place while Divorce Rates increase.
- ✓ Promotion of and Increases in Common Law Relationships and Promiscuity
- ✓ Significant increase in abortion rates and dramatic rise in the sale of dead embryos and body parts.
- ✓ Less desire to gather as the Church as the zeal for God slowly dies.
- ✓ Greed, sexual perversion, witchcraft, high levels of dishonor and lack of care for another become rampant in society.

It is dangerous when God begins to give over the nation to their sinful practices, because what you desire is what you will get, including the repercussions that come along with it. Those repercussions include having leaders over the nation that will take away the nation's liberties.

Nations Are Born, Nations Die

Ecclesiastes 3: 1 – 2 says, *"To everything there is a season, a time for every purpose under heaven: A time to be born, and a time to die …"*

The decisions of every nation – morally and spiritually – will determine whether that nation lives or dies. Many nations in Europe and Asia are now dying. Surprisingly, many in the Caribbean have been and are still trying to be like those nations. When natural laws are broken there are always consequences. Likewise, the same goes for spiritual laws, and the impact for that is more far-reaching than anyone can imagine.

When the institution of Family begins to breakdown, that is the beginning of moral and spiritual collapse. Transformation and restoration of moral and spiritual collapse can only come through the Holy Spirit of God. It starts with repentance, prayer, fasting, prophesying – speaking the messages from God – not from man nor to please man, and spiritual cleansing according to Ezekiel 36 – so that God will give new hearts and new desires. Transformation happens from the inside out; and only God can bring transformation in a nation. Most want transformation by way of conforming to the blueprints of other nations. However, that would only propel greater moral and spiritual decline.

We have seen the political Ferris wheel in effect decade after decade in our nation with no effort to change. We continue to hear the big promises with little result. We hear of fancy forecasts and plans to bring change for the better, and we must come to the realization that it is all talk and no action.

Sir Winston Churchill once said, "Politics is the ability to foretell what is going to happen tomorrow, next week, next month and next year. And to have the ability afterwards to explain why it didn't happen." This is what we see happening in our society.

Winston Churchill said, "The one thing we have learned from history is that we don't learn from history."
However, I implore us all to learn from history and prepare for a great overturn.

Chapter 7

FATHERS LEADING THE CHANGE

We have been seeing crises everywhere – school shootings, gang violence, the breakdown of morals in society, and it is all leading back to the absence of fathers. The prisons are being filled because of the absence of the fathers. As we conduct marriage and family counseling, we recognize that the absence of the father is one of the main contributors to the problem. Surprisingly, while families are broken, there is a lot of money being given by First World countries to come against the family institution in general. Furthermore, the media and the radical feminists are working around the clock to remove fathers from the society. The time is now for fathers rise up and align themselves right and bring change to the society.

Unfortunately, many fathers do not know their role; even more so, many husbands don't know their roles either. 1 Corinthians 4: 15 – 17 reminds us, *"For though you might have ten thousand instructors in Christ, yet you do not have many fathers; for in Christ Jesus, I have begotten you through the gospel. Therefore, I urge you, imitate me."*

It is critical to look at this scripture as a lack of good fathers is preventing growth and development and maturity, both within the world and in the Church and as a result there is a crisis regarding leadership for the next generation.

True fathers birth sons and daughters, not just spiritually, but physically. They also motivate their children, and they carry a key to unlock one's true potential – bringing maturity to those they father.

We are now seeing the signs of a fatherless generation.

A Father Must Be A Father

Bringing forth a child is not the only qualification for fatherhood. They must cover, provide for, discipline, impart to, mentor and encourage. Their words have capacity to bring forth life and death – blessings or curses.

We see in the Bible that each time an important milestone was reached in the life of Jesus, the Father always spoke. Fathers give assurance, confidence, and healing to those who suffer from rejection – particularly the girls. They can shift the atmosphere at any time bringing in order where there is disorder, as well as alignment where things are awry and will also bring accountability.

Very rarely do we see good fathers rising with truth. The father is the one who teaches their children to fear God as well as discipline and respect. The words of a father can decide the way of a child or the length of their days.

The true father also teaches their children the power of prayer, forgiveness, the Word of God. Furthermore, they don't provoke their children to anger, but instead discipline them God's way. Malachi 4: 5-6 outlines that there has to be a restoration of the fathers to the children.

This scripture lets us recognize that the hearts of the fathers were first turned from their children and as a result the hearts of the children were then turned away from their fathers. So, if there is to be any change within society and by extension the world, then the hearts of the fathers must first be turned back to their children and the hearts of the children will be turned back to their fathers. This scripture also reminds us that this is also the solution for climate change.

Every climate change expert should know that unless the restoration of the relationship between fathers and their children takes place then the climatic crises will continue.

A Good Father

A good father leaves a legacy for their children. Legacy is not just money but also a spiritual foundation; and that brings generational blessings. They are also always accessible to their children. They also pray for their children daily. (Jeremiah 33: 3, 1 Samuel 12: 23). They promote unity and will not permit strife in their house. They will not cease believing in their children.

When there are no good fathers, the dons become the fathers, then we have problems in society. Proverbs 23: 24

is the key to how we treat fathers and mothers; every child should respect that or be taught to respect that. They should never allow anyone to dictate otherwise to them.

Another thing that children need to be taught is that there is great danger when they disrespect or dishonor their fathers, because according to Exodus 20: 12 and Matthew 15: 4, that act determines the length of their days.

A good father always shows compassion to their children, according to Psalm 103: 13.

Every father should know, and so should everyone else, that fathers are to be the representatives of the Heavenly Father here on earth, hence, we are not supposed to compromise or seek to be politically correct, because we are made in His image.

Hence they are not to be afraid of disciplining their sons and daughters.

Fathers Do Not Forfeit Your Priesthood

With all the problems the nation is undergoing right now, including the disorder that is evident, it is an indication that there is a national crisis brewing.
The nation needs fathers.

The father functions as the priest for the family, and the reason there are so many problems is there is an absence of godly priests in the home instructing the children. So, if there is going to be any drastic changes in the nation there has to be the restoration of Godly fathers.

While mothers are extremely important and hold a treasured place in our hearts and homes, a mother cannot do a father's role in its entirety.

God's original order was for fathers to lead and walk in godly authority. Furthermore, we cannot use gender issues to change that fact.

The reason women have had to play the dual role of mother and father in the home is that some of the men have forfeited their priesthood; and we are now seeing its effect play out in our nation through the high levels of crime, violence, political tribalism, lack of order, indiscipline and other social issues.

The foundation on which a father stands determines the success of his family and, in particular, of his children. A father is a teacher, advisor, and counselor. They are responsible for instilling discipline in their children. They tell them the truth and motivate them. They encourage them and teach them about the power of forgiveness. (Ephesians 4:32) They transfer the inheritance blessing in the lives of their children. A simple laying of hands on their children daily while speaking blessings over them can change their circumstances and bring them into the path of success.

The father must pray in the hearing of their children and teach them to pray. (I Samuel 12: 23; Ephesians 6: 4)

Check Our Leaders

If you want to know why we are in a political crisis, check how many of our national leaders across the sectors had good relationships with their fathers; were accepted by their fathers; and had their fathers' influence throughout their lives.

While this issue is deeply personal and can be a 'touchy' issue for many, we must recognize that unless that cycle is broken, then there are serious problems ahead. We need fathers to break the cycle from their children. Cycles such as:

Rejection - many fathers rejected their children even before they were born.

Hereditary illnesses - fathers have a godly authority to speak healing over their children.

Rape and abuse - too many children are being abused, raped, and killed. Fathers must stand up against that issue.

Lack of forgiveness - it is the father who must show love, affection, and approval to their children.

The collapse and failure of marriages and families are because of the marriages taking place without the blessing of the fathers. If we study the Bible carefully, marriage should not take place without the blessing of the father. The father is the covering, and as we all know, where there is no roof, we become exposed to the elements - false doctrines, deceptions, and sexual predators.

We may need to do some research on those who are imprisoned and find out how many of them had a father present when they were growing up. We might be surprised at the results. This is not to say that those with both parents present are incapable of doing wrong, but there is significance to having a father present in the lives of their children. Even if we should speak to the most hard-hearted murderer, once you touch the issue of their fathers, they break down.

The lack of effectiveness of some of the church leaders is as a result of the lack of fathers in the church to mentor and motivate sons and daughters to fulfil their purpose. A person can be a pastor, but not a father!

A real father can turn a failing individual - sports personality, student, husband - into a success, just by being a father to them.

If we are going to look at dealing with crime seriously, then we will have to get judges, lawyers, police and godly leaders (not necessarily pastors) who are good fathers, to bring change.

Time For Fathers To Stand

Anything God creates in perfect order there is always a fight to bring disorder and to remove it from the purpose and position God has placed it.

For years, fathers have been under great attack, especially from high places and places of influence. The time has come for fathers to be restored and repositioned in society and in the lives of their children.

There are very few political administrations, locally and globally, who have done anything significant or effective to restore fathers to their rightful position. Instead, the focus seems to be solely on women and girls. This kind of instability has caused great pain to the family. When the family is not aligned, the nation is not aligned. Everything else will be out of alignment.

There are many reports that have been done globally. Almost 75 per cent of children who are living in fatherless households will experience poverty before the age of 11, compared with only 20 per cent in households with both parents.

Children living in homes where fathers are absent are more likely to be expelled from or drop out of school, develop behavioral problems, commit suicide, or fall victim to child abuse. They also make up 70 per cent of the prison population. So, the question is, if the absence of fathers brings so many problems to our personal and national existence, why is there not more focus on restoring fathers, rather than focusing only on the development of women and girls? The other question is, what are we saying to our sons who are potential fathers? This is a crisis, and it is no secret that there is a well-funded, coordinated effort to destroy the patriarchal position within society.

An attack on the fathers is an attack on the heavenly Father. Furthermore, it is an attack to destroy the family. Many media houses, globally, promote the assault on fathers. In some countries, fathers are excluded from certain welfare systems and shelters when they fall on hard times.

Why The Attack On Fathers?

The attack on fathers is an assault on what being a father represents: godly authority. Fathers bless, cover, protect and discipline, and when we remove the head from the body, the family dies. Our daughters are abused, raped and used as guinea pigs. Our sons' true purposes perish, as they are brainwashed into views and activities that they were not created to embrace. An attack on the fathers is an attack on creation, and on the instructions that God gave in Genesis 1: 26 – 28.

The negative treatment of fathers is an offensive on conception, godly offspring, and the Church, and the goal is to reduce mankind's authority to have dominion in the earth and confront satanic forces. God created man to subdue the earth and have dominion over it and stop satanic advances in the earth.

The constant criticism of fathers is also designed to create a division to come against the unity God created between male and female. The enemy knows the power of unity and most families fall because there is no unity. A united family stops the advancement of satanic forces. So, the enemy is creating division with his gender agenda.

The attack on fathers also has to do with removing/shifting birthright from the children and the generation to come, and it also has to do with creating new norms for what we 'call' family. Fathers carry seeds to affect the law of multiplication. The Devil cannot reproduce. Why do you think there are so many attacks on the womb, especially where women are carrying male children?

Fathers And Children

Paul outlined that there are many teachers but not many fathers. We need fathers to bring children into maturity, and for mentorship and impartation. The absence of fathers is evident in our political and social arenas, as well as in the Church.

I encourage the women to motivate and encourage the men in their lives to take care of their children wherever they may be.

Fathers, recognize that a good father acknowledges and compliments their children when they do good things and encourage them to do good things, or to do the right things when they do wrong. Good fathers identify and acknowledge every milestone in their child's life and recognize that when they speak as fathers, change takes place.

Good Mothers

Good mothers possess the power to turn negatives into positives and uplift in the most challenging situations – they can change the course of a nation.

Builders

Good mothers build their foundations on the Word and prayer. They are strong, especially for their children and their husbands. They would never teach disrespect – instead they teach the value of honor and the importance of respect. They teach their children the value of forgiveness. They teach their children – especially their daughters – how to be independent and the value of a good education. Many mothers have told their daughters never to go out (especially on a date) without having their own money so they won't be held at ransom or left stranded.

Good mothers share with their children the things they have learned through both good and bad experiences. They teach both daughters and sons how to manage their household and when doing household chores, they do it with a song of encouragement.

Good mothers teach their children how to prepare their meals instead of living on 'fast food'. They always have something baked and put aside as a treat. Good mothers teach their children that clothes and shoes are not what determine their beauty, but that beauty lies within. They teach them the importance of dressing well/appropriately, and that how they carry themselves indicates their level of self-respect.

Teachers

Good mothers teach their children proper values and attitudes. They are teaching their sons not to become womanizers and drunkards because it will affect their judgment particularly if they enter the judicial and political arenas. They teach them to walk as kings.

Good mothers, as an example, don't take sides in a dispute or compromise with their children when they are wrong. They encourage their children, and by extension their husbands, to live up to their responsibilities when children are born out of infidelity or wedlock. Good mothers teach their children the importance of marriage and the dangers of common-law relationships and how it leads to poverty and disrespect. They will also exercise the gift of giving as an example to their children to do the same.

Good mothers understand creative financing and know how to turn one dollar into a hundred dollars. So, they teach their children, especially by example, how to be industrious and that instead of "putting all their eggs in one basket" they should have multiple streams of income and the value of saving. A good mother always has something set aside "under the mattress" for a rainy day and teaches her children to do the same.

Discerners

Good mothers are discerners. They warn their children against making wrong choices particularly in relationships and will show tough love when they are disrespected. Yet they are quick to forgive when there is repentance. They understand what it is to make sacrifices by putting their family's welfare ahead of their own.

Both Church and nation are now feeling the effects of not having enough good mothers to teach the value of holiness and living a consecrated lifestyle.

Wise

In times of adversity, good mothers know how to comfort; and many times, they will say, "God will make a way". They will not cease to stand with their children until they see the breakthrough. They possess the Fruit of the Spirit and will not tolerate gossip or malice among their children. They teach their children anger management and faith to fight for their dreams. They know the art of speaking positive words.

I believe that the community, civic society, and government should identify and recognize good mothers within the society and allow them the opportunity also to pass on their experience to other mothers. Local film makers and theater personnel need to bring out more material that highlights the value of good mothers and honor them as well.

Chapter 8

DEALING WITH INCEST AND SEXUAL ABUSE

Incest and sexual abuse are eating away at the society, and affecting many areas therein. Meanwhile many want to make it a gender issue, but it affects both genders and sadly, it affects more boys than many are willing to admit.

While there are efforts to bring to fruition a court that is specifically focused on those issues, we must deal with it from its root; and we cannot honor some sexual sins while we deride others – it must be dealt with from the root and we have to be truthful about it all.

Sexual Sins

Sexual sins are the product of the spirit of perversion, and perversion cannot be effectively dealt with by human logic, intellect, or opinion. It is like a contagious plague, and it brings defilement to nations, churches, families, and daily living. It even corrupts the bloodline and spiritual DNA. So, where there are those who may say that they are adults who can do whatever they want whenever and however they choose, it is not so. Everything we each do – regardless of how insignificant or private it may seem, it affects everyone.

When King David committed adultery, it affected the entire nation and opened the door for murder, incest, conspiracy and untimely death. When incest took place between his daughters and himself, it opened the door to the birth of the Moabites who became a warring faction.

I can guarantee that most of those involved in crime were born out of either a common-law relationship, rape or even through incest, and so they did not get the benefit of the family as God originally intended, nor did many of them have their fathers in their lives as they should, if at all. This is why we must seek to strengthen and rebuild the institution of marriage.

Abuse

Dealing with abuse or incest starts in the home. The statement "children should be seen and not heard" has done a lot of damage in our society. Parents should listen to the things their children tell them and investigate it especially when they say someone has touched them inappropriately - whether it is Pastor, Teacher, relative, coach/P.E. teacher, doctor, visiting friend or the highly respected elder in the society. Furthermore, the church is not exempt from issues because imperfect people go to church and sadly there are many who sit on the church board, committees or even sit in the pews who fear neither God nor man, and consider the church their playground. So we need to stop blaming God when these things happen and start taking responsibility – start paying closer attention to our children. We need to stop covering some sexual sins while seeking to expose others; we need to stop trying to discredit some schools while we cover up the other because of the names of those who have children attending the school.

Schools

All the teachers in the schools must be trained to discern/identify where abuse exists and where children are abused/hurting. We need to stop shoving the truth under the "psychological rug" and stop trying to categorize these issues at the expense of our children's mental, emotional and spiritual welfare.

The teachers of today must also seek to **be** the good examples that their students should follow – especially in their dress, manners/attitude and mannerisms. Furthermore, we cannot honor one genre of music and its style of dance and attire while we condemn another when they both do the same thing and yield the same results. For example, Dancehall vs Carnival.

In addition to that, we cannot promote abortion, masturbation and oral sex in public, for example, while we have an outcry against pedophilia and allow our children onto the internet unsupervised and open to all kinds of pornography and graphic images sending them into a downward spiral of skewed emotions, mental states and thought patterns.

God Wants To Heal

There are many people whose lives have been shattered and they have become bitter, angry, unforgiving and hurt. But we must recognize that healing begins with forgiveness. It is not the person, but the spirit behind their actions/behavior. Some people genuinely don't know how to deal with it or how to respond to care, affection or kindness.

God wants to bring healing to those directly and indirectly affected by these issues and He wants those whom He has delivered from these painful experiences to come forward and tell their story so that others can be healed by their testimony. They must no longer be ashamed because our mess oftentimes becomes our message and ministry.

Recognize that true and complete healing cannot take place until there is forgiveness. Then your message will have power.

Abortion Creating A Global Vacuum

Globally, we are crying out for visionaries and righteous leaders in various sectors to solve the issues that now exist globally. But most of the problems that need to be solved globally have occurred as a result of the vacuum created by abortion. God created each person to bring solutions to issues that He knew would arise because of man's selfishness.

As is revealed in the Scriptures – Jeremiah 1: 5, Galatians 1: 15 and Psalm 139: 13 – God's purpose and assignments begins once there is conception.

The issue of Therapeutic/Elective Abortion is an issue which is quite controversial today. Many say it is a woman's right for her to determine what she wants to do with her own body. But this is exactly the kind of deception that is running rampant throughout nations.

I Corinthians 6: 18 – 20 reminds us that God dwells in our temples. Abortion destroys your physical and spiritual bodies and has the potential to cause great emotional and spiritual damage in the future. In the same way that when the natural laws are broken there are legal consequences, likewise, when Spiritual Laws are broken, it opens the door for other things to happen personally and in the wider society.

Today we are seeing the residual effects of abortion as it affects our nations. How so? Abortion opens the door to untimely deaths, violence, crime, as well as the eradication of purpose, vision and ideas for all sectors.

From the beginning of time, everything we do individually, affects the world entirely. Our personal choices have caused climate changes, environmental shifts, increased deaths, diminished values and so much more. (Genesis 3: 17) So that sometimes when we think that we are getting rid of a potential problem, we are in fact creating bigger ones.

What if the purposes of certain well-known people in the numerous sectors were never brought to light because of abortion? What if the great men and women of the past and of today, who were raised by single parents, never existed because of abortion? What if there was no Bob Marley, no Martin Luther King Jr or no Nelson Mandela? We would never have the benefit of their gifts, talents and expertise; and whatever impact they have made would never have been!

Some nations are using legislation to force women to abort their girls. What if the nations did not have the benefit of some of the great women of the past and present. What if there was no Florence Nightingale, Marie Curie or Mother Teresa? All these women contributed immensely to sensitizing the nations to issues such as poverty, health, justice, and science and made significant impact on Global Laws and Economies.

What Nations Should Do

Reduce the funds/funding being spent on abortions and give those to Humanitarian Groups and NGOs who will educate, empower and enrich the lives of the poor and neglected ones worldwide.

Relax adoption laws that hinder those who genuinely qualify to keep the children who are unwanted by their natural parents. Help those who want to adopt, regardless of their income level, to be able to do so and make a positive difference in the lives of unplanned children. It cannot be easier to abort a child, rather than to adopt one! It's not right.

In a study done of the United States in 2012, the following was revealed.

50% of U.S. women obtaining abortions are younger than 25; women aged 20-24 obtain 33% of all U.S. abortions and teenagers obtain 17%

In 2009, adolescents under 15 years obtained .05% of all abortions, but had the highest abortion ratio, 785 abortions for every 1,000 live births

Black women are more than 4.8 times more likely than non-Hispanic white women to have an abortion and Hispanic women are 2.7 times as likely

In 2009, 85% of all abortions were performed on unmarried women

Among women who obtained abortions in 2009, 40.2% had no prior live births; 46.3% had one or two prior live births, and 13.6% had three or more prior live births

If this is so for one nation, what is happening in your nation, under your noses – without our knowledge? What valuable resources are the nations - and even our own lives - lacking when abortions are performed?

Food for thought.

Prayer For The Unborn Child/Children

Pray this prayer 3 times daily and ask the Lord to release angels to protect the unborn. Regardless of what the naysayers say, life begins in the womb. It is imperative for us to pray daily the Word of God over the unborn child. Ask the Lord to put a hedge of protection around the unborn child, the mother and that entire family during that season. Ask the Lord to fill the child with His Holy Spirit and cover the child with the Blood of Jesus. Pray that the Lord will strengthen the uterus, cervix and that there will be normal sugar and blood pressure levels at all times. Ask the Lord to drive away any and every abnormality, curse and any negative words spoken against you. Pray against every attack from ancestral spirits, spirits of infirmities, stress and any diabolical spirits coming against you. Drink a lot of water. Anoint your belly daily and play music that worships God. The unborn child can hear while they are in the womb. (Luke 1: 39 – 45 & 46 – 56).

Father in the name of Jesus, I come to you Lord for protection, strength and wisdom for my unborn child (insert child's name here if you have one…). Behold children are an heritage from the Lord. The fruit of the womb is a reward. Like arrows in the hands of a warrior, so are the children of our youth. (Psalms 127: 3 – 4)
Know ye that the Lord, He is God. It is He Who has made us and not we ourselves. We are His people and the sheep

of His Pasture; and because of that, we ask you Lord to put on the whole armor upon this child. The helmet of salvation, the breastplate of righteousness, the shield of faith; the Sword of the Spirit – which is the word of God. Gird their loins with truth; shod their feet with the preparation of the Gospel of Peace. This child shall grow from strength to strength, wealth to wealth, increase in wisdom.

Psalm 139: 13 reminds us – "For You formed my inward parts; You covered me in my mother's womb." Father I thank you for daily favor and development. Cover me going out and coming in. Cover me from accidents and incidents. Give me favor with doctors, nurses, insurance companies, the government and let your angels rally around us 24/7. Cover every detail, purpose and assignment of my life from the enemy.

Help me to stay in your word daily and remove every potential depression and discouragement that may seek to attack me and my family in Jesus' Name. Amen

Read also:

Jeremiah 1: 5, Isaiah 44: 24, Isaiah 64: 8, Galatians 1: 15, Luke 2: 67, Ephesians 1: 3 – 4, Deuteronomy 7: 13, Genesis 49: 25 and Job 31: 15.

The Bastard Curse

Deuteronomy 23: 2 says, *"One of illegitimate birth shall not enter the assembly of the Lord; even to the tenth generation none of his descendants shall enter the assembly of the Lord."*

A *"bastard"* is defined *"a person born of parents not married to each other; illegitimate child; anything inferior or varying from standard; (being) of illegitimate birth or of uncertain origin."*

According to Deuteronomy 23: 2, the *Bastard Curse* is real. This curse has affected many nations and cultures, in particular the Black and Hispanic peoples, and it brings along with it rejection, bitterness, hatred, rebellion and lust. As a result, many children are born out of wedlock, people committing abortion and fathers who refuse to accept and embrace their children.

This curse will attack a lineage and can also create great poverty within an entire nation. We have seen countries trying to pass laws in order to make the Bastard Curse seem unreal especially as it relates to inheritance, but the breaking of Spiritual laws is real; and a nation or a community cannot be free until the Bastard Curse is broken. We must recognize, however, that this curse cannot be broken by way of the legal framework but can only be rectified Spiritually and with Divine intervention.

Most people under the bastard curse find it difficult to get married or to have children without having the experience of a miscarriage. The bastard curse brings many negative experiences in families and nations, it increases crime and violence and causes great suffering. We need to begin to examine those on drugs and those involved in witchcraft, tattoos, and prostitution to see their connection to the Bastard Curse. Furthermore, according to an article titled, "The Consequences of Fatherlessness", surveys have shown that "…children from fatherless homes are more likely to be poor, become involved in drug and alcohol abuse, drop out of school, and suffer from health and emotional problems. Boys are more likely to become involved in crime, and girls are more likely to become pregnant as teens." These in addition to many of the societal issues faced by countries today are often the result of the Bastard Curse. (2 Samuel 11: 2 – 5).

When a child is conceived through adultery it opens the door for incest, murder, rape, conspiracy and pain, and can follow up to ten generations. Look at what happened to King David's administration, his children and family, as a result of the adultery he committed.

The Church is not exempt from the effects of the Bastard Curse, because it affects church growth and causes instability. There are many persons who constantly change churches, unable to settle down. If you should check the information, they were born out of wedlock and were rejected by their fathers, whether spiritual or biological.

Further to this, Abortion is another issue that stems from the Bastard Curse, and it is not only in relation to physical pregnancies, but it also affects us on a spiritual level - individually and nationally, because the whole issue of abortion is about terminating one's God-given purpose – the enemy's goal.

The Moabites, the lineage from which Ruth came, were conceived out of incest which brought a bastard curse; but through His sacrifice, Jesus Christ redeemed us from the curse of the law. God used Ruth to show, as He did with Jabez, that regardless of the curse, bastard or otherwise, Christ will break that curse when we accept him.

We need to begin to educate our children about the dangers of sex out of marriage, and of having children out of wedlock, as well as the dangers of incest and abortion. All these open the door for the Bastard Curse. Christ wants to destroy that Bastard Curse that has been robbing communities and nations.

If you were to check our prison population 70% of those within the prison were raise without a father in their lives because of the bastard curse. It is time for us to destroy that curse so the next generation may be free from the struggles, pain and suffering. We must pray aggressively for this curse to be broken.

Prayer To Break The Bastard Curse

Father, in the name of Jesus, I ask for Your forgiveness from ten generations for myself and my family. We stand on Galatians 3:13. We put all curses associated with the bastard curse that are coming against my purpose whether it be abortion, natural or spiritual, murder, death, incest, lust, rejection, failure at the edge of miracle, alcohol, hatred, bitterness, rejection. We ask you Jesus, to wipe away all sins and curses, every red circle against my name and every opposition to the fulfillment of my purpose. I replace it with God's grace, and we renounce the Bastard Curse, we take back all legal rights from the enemy. We close all demonic portals. We erase and delete all satanic records from the past regarding any affairs of my life, and we speak new beginning for us in Jesus' name. Remove any blockage known and unknown, any legal rights and I command that I begin to advance. Lord, I break the Bastard Curses now from my life. Lord, begin to enlarge my territory as you did for Jabez in Jesus name (2 Chronicles 4:10). We renounce and ask you to remove all legal rights and covenants in Jesus' name; and we thank you Lord for victory as you cleanse my spiritual DNA with your blood. We declare that the enemy will no longer block our progress and advancement, and there will be no more delay in Jesus' name. Amen.

Deliverance: The Children's Bread

Mark 7: 26 – 29 says, *"The woman was a Greek, a Syro-Phoenician by birth, and she kept asking Him to cast the demon out of her daughter. But Jesus said to her, "Let the children be filled first, for it is not good to take the children's bread and throw it to the little dogs." And she answered and said to Him, "Yes, Lord, yet even the little dogs under the table eat from the children's crumbs." Then He said to her, "For this saying go your way; the demon has gone out of your daughter."*

The recent happenings within the schools of Jamaica regarding the spiritual activities manifesting and the response to all of it, has revealed how low we have fallen spiritually as a nation, and sadly, in the Christian community. I was not surprised to hear a man of God come out against speaking in tongues in the school. We have gone so low spiritually, that this generation is paying the price. While we reduce our faith and our depth in God, the forces of darkness are now taking over.

The happenings in the schools has revealed an opportunity for us to rescue our generation and deal with the current spiritual condition and the healing of the family infrastructure that need to take place.
It seems as if every time the Lord gives us an opportunity, we reject it and choose the road of "40 years in the wilderness".

Corporate worship is relevant, not only in the House of God, but in every place we are together. Prayer must be everywhere, and it includes praying in the spirit. We cannot use protocol to come against the Spirit of God, He has His protocol. (Ephesians 6: 18)

Deliverance

It is critical for us to understand that deliverance ministry is real, relevant and is a miracle ministry. The Word tells us that we must cast out demons and set the captives free. Mark 16: 14 – 17 is a command from Jesus. Demons need a body as their host. Once they are given that legal right they will occupy.

Our present school system has been used by the enemy as an open door giving legal right to the enemy to attack our children in various ways. The things to which they listen, what they watch, what they are instructed to write and draw as self-expression, have succeeded in stealing the innocence of our children and youth. Some of the children have tattoos – serpent tattoos, some have been abused, raped and sold. There are immoral and perverse games they watch and dances in which they participate that are gates through which demonic possession comes. There are major organizations that spend millions for our children to get possessed. Have you ever listened to the lyrics of some of the songs they play? Some adults say they listen to the reggae songs the kids play but they don't take the time to really listen because they can't tolerate the beats. They need to listen to the other genre of music too.

When our own influential people in society encourage the youth to engage in masturbation but refuse to tell them to abstain from premarital sexual activity, then the door is open for demonic possession. Much of what they say is a mental health issue is in fact a demonic possession.

Learn From Mark 5

Mark 5 is a "teaching moment" for everyone. The region that Jesus entered was surrounded by darkness - the absence of light, which is the absence of God's Presence. Once there is that absence, then people will begin to get possessed demonically. It therefore means that we are opening the door to things like mass shooting in schools, increase in suicides, murders, disrespect to all authority.

The man in Mark 5 would have been deemed a Mental Health Case in our world today. However, He was possessed, hence his mind was not sound, he had super-human strength and the Jesus' Presence began to torment him.

So once a person is possessed and a Child of Light – a servant of God (male or female) is in their presence, you will see manifestation. When manifestation comes, it is critical to set them free. So the psychologists of today would have been treating this man for a psychological break down – maybe Chronic Schizophrenia – when in fact this man had 6000 demons in him – legion.

There are many of our youth today that are walking around with more than 6000 demons in them, and when any one of them cold-heartedly wipes a family out, what do you think is the issue?

Do We Truly Want Change

If we truly want change, then we need to stop diagnosing the issue incorrectly. Giving the wrong diagnosis worsens and increases the problem. It is also critical for those in authority to ensure that they seek people who understand the topic. (Isaiah 56: 10 – 11)

Our schools are crumbling, and it reflects what has happened in the family. Failing to apply the proper remedy for the various strongholds will create more chaos and death.

Save The Next Generation

Everything today is market-driven. Decisions are made based on the needs of the market.

Abortion and immorality are now in great demand. Abortion negatively affects business. If population decreases so will demand for goods and services, including real estate, loans, clothing, food, medical services and vehicles; thus population and demand are positively related.

Abortion is affecting the population growth. We are now seeing it negatively affect real estate and other businesses. When the family decreases, it affects the demand for certain kinds of properties.

Furthermore, it can significantly change the landscape of the construction industry.

Almost every organisation uses market trends to make business decisions and most businesspersons are now jumping on the bandwagon because, to them, there is a great change towards people who want to engage in abortions, witchcraft and immorality.

Media and government are also heavily involved in the change in market trends and their decisions are based on current trends. As a result, they are also going with the flow of the tide. So, there is no longer accountability or new ideas, and, as such, the word for the moment is 'let's give the people what they want.'

Threats To Humanity

On that basis, politicians are no longer being held accountable. What is going to happen when the current trend changes; because one of life's constants is change?

Abortion and immorality are threats to humanity. While many companies within the various industries will benefit from this trend - pharmaceutical industry, medical industries, the gaming industries, politicians, activists and the entertainment industry.

Abortion eliminates the true visionaries and creates a global vacuum. Geniuses and those with solutions for the problems, and it is a threat to Christianity.

Here's a thought. If other religions don't accept abortion, but Christians and the Christian nations do, what will that do to Christianity and the Christian population; or is that the plan?

In addition to this, studies have shown that most of the abortions are done by black people. Many of the places that conduct abortions are within or close to black communities. Do the checks.

Could this be an effort to significantly diminish the black race? Why is abortion being pushed as an alternative for family planning, for developing nations? It is interesting that many of our top athletes and game changers come from developing nations.

What is to become of the global society if abortion becomes the order of the day?

Our universities have now become the testing labs and 'porn shops' for those testing 'market theories' and needing guinea pigs for their experiments. The universities that ought to be churning out the leaders of tomorrow have become the launch pad for immorality, lewd behavior and less-than-desirable attitudes.

God's Property

Many have come forward to declare that people should make their own decisions about their own bodies. But this is somewhat a deception. First and foremost is the fact that our bodies are God's property. Our bodies are the temple of the Holy Spirit and, as such, should be respected and treated the way He sees fit.

Additionally, Psalm 127: 3 – 4 says children are a heritage from the Lord. So, regardless of the way in which they have come about, some children may be unplanned, but they are not unwanted. They are the next prime minister, then next beauty queen, the next track legend.

The Bible describes anything that has blood as having life. By day 22 of pregnancy, a fetus' heart begins to beat with its own blood. So, by the time most women realize they are pregnant the heart of their fetus is beating, and it means they have life.

Research shows approximately 10 per cent of all legal abortions end with one or more of the following complications – accidental tearing, tearing of the cervix, perforation of the uterus, heavy bleeding, miscarriage of future pregnancies, increased risk of subsequent tubal pregnancies, damage of internal organs, hepatitis, blood clots, sterility and death. This does not include the psychological effects that abortion can have On those involved.

Let's save the next generation!

My Right To Be Pro-Life

Everybody is talking about rights. But rights without the right foundation causes us to make wrong choices. Jesus gave His life for us all to have life. Ladies, God gave you a womb to bring life! never allow your womb to be used to do something for which God did not create it to be. Your body is the temple of the Holy Spirit and the only place the Holy Spirit does not dwell is in a cemetery. Don't let anyone use you for population control. If the statistics show that it is mainly Black and Hispanic people with strong Christian beliefs that are being "encouraged" to exercise their reproductive rights (do abortions) what then will become to our peoples? Just as it was with the Israelites, it is being said that these peoples (Black and Hispanic) are becoming too strong - they are not the minorities they once were.

It is interesting that China and India have the largest population in the world, and while there are rigid attempts to control China's population, there is no reference to them being "too strong" - meanwhile the Chinese are everywhere. Nigeria and Brazil are the only Black and Hispanic nations among the top 10 highest population in the world. Could the lack of a similar outcry against China and India be because the rest of the World can benefit from their manufacturing prowess? or because of the prowess of the Indians in Science, Technology, and the fact that there is gold in abundance there? Could it possibly be that they would want to take control of the land and the gold that exist in the Third World nations? Or are the after the existence of the Nuclear Family or Christian values? Can they go into Muslim nations and tell them to use birth control or have abortions?

If we truly cared about our women, why not empower our women and give them hope, assist in education for them and their children. And if there is an unplanned pregnancy, why not give assistance by relaxing the adoption laws for example? Why not teach abstinence rather than abortion? Why is it easier to get money for abortion than it is to get money for education.

I declare that multiplication regarding having children will come upon all married couples today and are struggling with that issue. And I declare that all who have done abortions in the past are healed and delivered.

I have a right to be **Pro-Life** because Proverbs 31: 8 tells me **"Open Your Mouth For The Speechless, In The Cause Of All Who Are Appointed To Die"**

Change, Children And Communication

With the worldwide crises now affecting children, many are giving different opinions on what is to be done, some blame parenting skills. What we are realizing is that a parent cannot impart what they themselves have never experienced. So, we now must rebuild the foundation and build it on and with truth.

There are many 'truths' in this world today, but there is only one right truth – Proverbs 16: 25 and Proverbs 14: 12. It is all our duty to win our youth over from philosophical views. They must be made to understand that man's views, wisdom, or reasoning is superior to God's! (Colossians 2: 8) We need to teach our youth how to deal with/handle subtle reasoning – Colossians 2: 4 – that would steer them away from the Truth.

There are many 'lights' in this world, and the enemy seeks out brilliant, intellectual, powerful and popular people that he can influence and use, to reach others in order to influence their way of thinking. The failure of the church leaders over the years is that they were diluting the truth to facilitate this generation because they did not know how to deal with them; neither did they have a new revelation of the Word itself. So they have abandoned the 'Old Gate'

(Nehemiah 3) and have allowed New Age philosophies to infiltrate our youth. We are bringing in these new philosophies and Hollywood syndrome to suit the desires of man. So, when popular or powerful people engage in less than wholesome activities or brazenly engage in sinful activities, these actions are glamorized and are used to pull on the emotions of the public; thus belittling or ignoring the truth of the situation – that it is wrong!

'Children' Includes Boys

According to Gleaner article entitled "Women Shouldn't Lower Standards For Men – Students" dated November 15, 2012, the Economic and Social Survey showed that most of those dropping out of school and being incarcerated today are boys. It stated **"...the survey also shows that of the 1,937 persons who entered correctional institutions in Jamaica last year, males accounted for 1,748 or 90 per cent of that number."**

Clearly the boys are being neglected by the society in general. The men were created as the covering for the females; so as a result, they are open to more direct attacks to destroy them. If they go to prison or are slaughtered, then the society becomes imbalanced.

In the classrooms, there is a female-teacher majority, and they teach both boys and girls. Within a society it is the man/father who ought to carry out the discipline within the family. So herein lies the problem, there are very few men to help maintain and execute the disciplining and to deal with male-specific issues when they arise. Today, more males being raped and abused in the society – some even experience this from an early age. Then, instead of dealing with the issues on both sides and bring balance to the situation overall, there is greater focus on the issue of gender – women and girls – than there is on making the society safe for boys and girls to live, learn and grow.

There are often discussions on the issue of Women and Children, but as it concerns the issue of 'Children' it usually focuses on girls and neglects the boys within the society; but 'Children' includes boys too. If that neglect continues, then where are the girls going to get husbands – or is that the plan? Furthermore, we cannot exclude the fathers; good ones still exist.

Communication

If we are going to change society, then we will need to change what we are putting out in the environment – both local and global media will need revamping and added value to their public offerings. Many of the media houses are focusing on the dollar value and the negative things. For example, sex sells! Conflict grabs attention! Disrespect and dishonor are revered! But all these are negatively impacting the economy, the social fabric of the nation and are destroying our children.

Some media houses and production companies are not even supporting or producing programs that are family oriented. Sadly, fabricated 'Reality' shows are taking over the networks.

Some don't even believe that God is necessary to the environment and in our daily affairs. The general view and perception of the Church and the Holy Scriptures are that those in the Church are money-hungry simpletons who are oblivious to the issues at hand and that the Bible is irrelevant.

The media has a mandate to bring positive changes globally. Negative words shape, change or bring down a society. (James 3: 5 – 11; Isaiah 52: 7; Philippians 4: 8)

Examining Education

It is critical for us to scrutinize all sources of information that are becoming a part of the education process. If one source of information is flawed or deceptive, and lacks foundational truths, what kind of society are we developing.

In using uncleanness, lies and backward thinking as the foundation for educating our society today, we have set a dangerous precedent and as it stands many are unable to bring solutions to the table concerning crime, health, economics, and justice.

We are now reaping the harvest. If we are in an era where there are more educated people, why are we then struggling for solutions?

Education without the involvement of the Holy Spirit causes a person to be limited in every way. That is why we need the Spirit of Truth, as in Ephesians 1, and the Spirit of

Wisdom and Revelation, to reveal the mysteries of God's Creation – Ephesians 1: 17.

There are too many who have conformed to the world, but very little transformation has been taking place, and that creates unnecessary cycles! There are no solutions coming forth – only violence, mechanisms for bondage and oppression.

Very shortly, we will see more lock downs, more starvation, more breakdowns and more lies. We seem to have gone back to the days of the pirates. The very people who are saying the Bible is not real, are fighting to promote the very thing the Bible says they would be promoting – one world religion, one world currency, cashless society, forced vaccination especially upon travelers, promotion and the increase in the use of AI (Artificial Intelligence) and forced medicals, smart cities and a militarized nation.

Those who are usually vocal against Christianity, are silent against the real issues and problems. They preferred to be ruled by evil rather than fight for good.

Chapter 9

MORE TRAINING FOR PARENTS NOT CRITICISMS

These days, there is a great deal of focus and negative criticism regarding parents and their parenting skills. Social Media and Mainstream Media are abuzz, particularly since so much has been happening to children lately.

Constructive Criticism

Constructive criticism must always be accompanied by solutions to do it better. Most in our society today are quick to offer criticism but have no workable solutions. Very few can tell you how to do a thing but are excellent "faultfinders". Some criticize simply to display their knowledge and how much better they think they are at the subject. They want to show the shortcomings of others. Many are critical of parents today, but how much better are they when in our society today, children are having children. Many talk about the failures of parents, but who is training them how to be successful? For some who may have the know-how it is all about money – so they charge a fee to pass on the information to those in need of help.

In some cases, within our classrooms today, children are teaching our children. So even their responses to situations that occur within the classroom are lacking in maturity.

Training Versus Teaching

Proverbs 22: 6 reminds us to train our children in the way they should go. The key word is to "train" not "teach" so it goes beyond imparting academic knowledge and includes wisdom, love, nurture, discipline and seeking to train according to the personality, gifts and aspirations of the child. In addition to all they are taught, they must be taught to be totally committed to God and steer clear of embracing other gods.

Titus 2 says the older women must teach the younger women and that the men are responsible for training the young men in the society. Furthermore, it says they must be taught proper values and attitudes, the importance of maintaining good character. Many times, we see popular people being brought in to influence the morals, values and the ways of thinking of our youth, when they themselves need to be mentored and trained. We must recognize the popularity is not a synonym for good values.

We must train young/new parents especially, how to identify dangerous and destructive habits, mindsets, attitudes, methods, as well as personalities that can destroy their children and stop them from accomplishing their purpose. Recognize two things – a good education has its foundations at home; and the fear of the Lord is the beginning of wisdom. Children learn leadership, responsibility, accountability, good values, biblically-based morals and love at home, and it starts with the parents.

Embracing The Right Principles

Parents must ensure that their children are eating from the right tree – the right source – in order to ensure their spiritual safety and development. Biblical principles outline two (2) trees in the Garden (Genesis 2: 9), so it is key to know the source of our children's knowledge within society; for every child we lose, we also lose a great deal of significant resources.

Invest In Their Future

It is very important for parents to invest in the future of their children, not only in terms of paying for their education, but also by preserving their quality of life by knowing and understanding what threats there are vying for their attention and protecting them from harm.

As it stands today, 22% of kids between the ages of 6 and 9 own cell phones? When they become tweens (9-12) it rises to 60%! This means even if your kids don't have cell phones, some of their friends probably already have them. There are Apps (Applications) that are developed with that age group in mind which pull their attention away from face-to-face interaction with their parents. Parents need to be aware of this and know that there are some very dangerous Apps which parents need to ensure their children avoid, because they endanger the lives of our children in many ways.

We need to set up centers to train parents and children on:
- ✓ The importance and value of money. (How not to waste it)
- ✓ Values and Attitudes
- ✓ Independence, Self-Reliance, and Entrepreneurship
- ✓ Abstinence and the Importance of Marriage

Exercise Parental Rights

The rights of parents are coming under attack. There are international stakeholders that want to diminish the rights of parents. It is critical for parents to know the God-given rights and authority they have as parents and that they are responsible for that and are accountable to God. God also warned in His word that the type of parenting one displays can determine the life span of a parent on earth. (Deuteronomy 11: 19 – 21; Deuteronomy 6: 7 and Proverbs 22: 6). There are even specific terminologies and meanings that people want to change in order to facilitate and support their diabolical plans to rob parents of their parental rights and authorities.

What Parents Can Do

First and foremost, you cannot be an effective parent without God's help.

Always set an example that your children can follow. They do what we do.

Always be vigilant and look for signs of abuse and depression, and even bullying at school. As soon as you identify these signs, you need to seek help, especially since there are many students today contemplating suicide. Part of this comes from the exposure they are getting to things like marijuana, immoral activities – some get pressured by all sexes. So, it is critical to pray the word of God over them daily.

As parents, you must always create a climate for open dialogue – where there can be dialogue without fear to address their problems. Also, ensure that the climate that exists within your home will not negatively affect them to the point that they want to run away from home.

Don't Compromise

Never compromise with your children. Remember that you are their parents, not their friend.

Parents must always know the whereabouts of their children and know their friends as well. Spend less time on social media and use that time to bond with your children.

Get involved with the Parent Teachers' Association and do spot checks on their curriculum so you know what they are being taught.

Parents, don't be afraid to hug your children – especially the boys; and speak life and the fulfillment of their purpose over them every day.

Never try to make your children into what you wanted to be; let them be whom God has said they are to be.

Always seek God for the name of your child, and how to grow them in relation to their purpose. Teach them about morals, values, how to dress. The world has more than enough half-naked people running around and does not need any more. Remind them that everything on or in this earth that is precious is always covered.

Teach your children about the fact that God made them perfect – so they don't need to bleach, darken, tattoo, pierce various body parts or anything of that nature because they were made well.

Teach them about the power of submission and how it for their protection more than anything else.

As parents, you must lead by example, and whatever you expect of them must begin with you first. Never teach them hate, teach them the power of forgiveness. Teach them the word of God and how to pray and to stay away from witchcraft and any other things that are not the principles and the instructions of God.

Never "poison" your children against another person – especially the other parent.

Teach them to respect the Law, their elders, others within society and themselves and to stay away from alcoholic beverages and gambling.

Teach them (both male and female) to cook, clean and be entrepreneurial in their endeavors.

Teach them how to join (and stay in) a line and how to be patriotic and to respect the flag and how to say "Yes ma'am" or "No Sir" when addressing other adults/elders.

Never discipline them when you are angry, and always explain to them the purpose of discipline.

Parents, remember, 90% of the problems in society has its roots in the home. You are the first line of authority. You are preparing leaders, husbands, wives and whatever you do is impacting society. The institution of the family today is broken and if we are going to bring change to that and ultimately to society, then it must begin in the home.

Know your rights and exercise them. Otherwise, then very shortly you will have no rights.

Family Problems Hurt Our Children

Your child is performing at the top of his/her class academically, and then suddenly, they start declining rapidly. This is just one of the many signs that problems exist in the home and/or the school.

It is critical for parents to discern the cause of the problems. Parents/Guardians, often blame the children without realizing that it may be their relationships between husband and wife, or other problems within the household that are affecting the child negatively. Children are very sensitive and what you think they don't know they know. For example, a parent may start coming in from work at later hours, or the parents are no longer sleeping in the same bedroom, or arguments increase and intensify, or a third party enters the equation and there is separation between the parents – or even where one parent goes outside of the marital relationship and has a child. What also affects the children is that one parent may lose their job and the lifestyle of the family changes and decline, and it affects them in many ways. So, while parents are focusing on their problems, the children are slipping through the cracks and are suffering. Some start joining gangs and getting into the wrong groups.

The Child Dynamic

Children become attached to things, relationships very easily - like the home they've always lived in, the community, church and even church building they have known since birth. So when drastic changes take place, there needs to be counseling because these issues that seem minor to adults, can go as far as leading to suicidal thoughts in the child/children. For some even losing a home affects a child so much that they hold on to it even into adulthood. Divorce affects our children far more than we think and so everything must be done to save the marriage. Contrary to popular belief, parents cannot afford to make big decisions independently they have to take the children into consideration because we cannot afford to produce cold-hearted killers. Our focus must change. While they have their place, gun control, growing an economy and making big agreements with financial giants – whether globally or locally – cannot be the sole or most important focus. Without strong familial structures on a national level, everything else we try to do will be in vain.

Parental Rules

Parents need to be careful about what they speak in the hearing of their children. Even the movies they watch in the home. The conversation they have about what is happening at work, at school or who they don't like at church affects the children and damages them emotionally, mentally and spiritually.

Parents must make time to have open discussion with their children to what concerns them and what is going on within them. They need also to establish a spiritual foundation where they read the Bible and pray for their children. Law makers must ensure that they do not force parents to be working on their day of worship – whether Saturday or Sunday - because this is destroying families and turning the hearts of our children cold and insensitive. New Age principles or tenets cannot replace the authentic Presence of God.

We have to understand that every decision that is made within a nation has an impact on and will affect our children. Even within a school, they are quicker to suspend or send the children home rather than seeking to find the root of the issue. There could be verbal or sexual abuse, or a breaking up of the family because of economic hardships. That is why there should be a greater emphasis on welfare – not just in terms of the financial aspect, but even more so regarding the human aspect of things. I hope one day to see the establishment of a Ministry of Family Affairs.

The Church

They need to begin to understand that the children are not secondary in the scheme of things, they are primary. We can't simply give them an iPad during service to occupy them while we get filled up. We need to utilize the Prophetic Gifting to minister to them in the same way we minister to adults, and deal with the hurting that is taking place within them.

Pray of the children each day for protection and remember, "…Children are a heritage from the Lord…" (Psalm 127: 3)

Invest In Your Children

We have seen a worldwide increase in the killings and untimely deaths of children. Further to this, we are seeing the gruesome deaths that snatch them away before and even after they are born.

We must understand that just as Herod and Pharaoh sought to kill the children in the days of old, it happens today! Herod and Pharaoh are not alive today, but the spirit of

Herod and the spirit of Pharaoh still want to destroy our children today. Each time that we see these killings and deaths increase it indicates that we are on the verge of a significant change.

Within each child conceived there is an instruction that can bring a positive change to the environment and nation to which they are born. The cure for cancer, the answer to the debt problem, the solution to a national crisis to come, or the answer to a current problem could be within any of our children; and if they are killed, those solutions go with them! How many solutions have we lost already? Remember Josiah? God can use children even from the age of eight (8).

Parents, the Government, the Church, the Schools, Non-Governmental Organizations (NGO's) and the Media need to re-evaluate their view and understanding of the importance of children in a nation! They need look at, how to teach them, how to bring out and encourage their gifts and talents, and how to invest in them; not just monetarily, but in every way!

The time has come for the nation to have a separate Ministry for Children and Family Affairs. It is one of the most important Ministries a nation needs, because without children, there is no continuation of or succession in the nation. The Lord once told me that 90% of the issues that exist now among leaders, including *'dons'*, start from their childhood! Some were raped, abused and for others their fathers never took care of them and they were never healed. As a result they and their decision-making are negatively affected.

What Are The Solutions

Teach them about the goodness of God morning, noon and night. There are benefits for doing so. (Deut. 6: 5 – 25; Deut. 4: 9 – 10)

Pray the whole armor of God over them daily. (Eph. 6: 10 - 20; Psalm 91)

Sow Seed, that is, give donations unto the Lord for your children. (Job 1: 1 – 5)

Spend time with them, learn about them and allow them to get to know you and your expectations of them.

Listen to them when they speak, do not push them away. Encourage them to talk to you. The old saying of *'children should be seen and not heard'* is not a Biblical Principle.'

Ensure that your children are dedicated to God (the Almighty) and anointed with Olive Oil, not just sprinkled with water; and also ensure that they are given Godly or Biblical names.

Speak *'life'* over them daily and declare what you want them to become. Death and life are in the power of the tongue. (Prov. 18: 21 – 22)

Teach the children about tithing, how to handle money and how to dress modestly – male and female. (Mal. 3: 8 – 10; Lev. 19; II Tim. 2: 9)

Parents must get to know the importance and significance of dreams and visions and let them report to you those dreams and visions that they are receiving.

Teach them about the Fruit of the Spirit. (Gal. 5: 22)

Hug your children and tell them you love them – even if you had never received that expression of love – use the opportunity to break that cycle.

Let them study at least one (1) business-related subject in secondary level school, it will help them understand basic economic principles.

Teach them to be vigilant when they enter tertiary level institutions – especially in choosing friends, movies, groups and so on.

Teach them about the dangers of sex outside of marriage, and the importance of seeking the Lord for their spouse.

Teach them about protocol in entering different environments and addressing different people.

Prayer For The Daily Protection Of Our Children

(Psalm 91, Psalm 121, Psalm 127:3-5)

Pray daily for coverage over our children from general accident and freak accident in our schools, daycare, playground etc.

The book of Job says we must pray and ask God to put a hedge of protection around our children daily. We must anoint them with oil and pray God's blessing and protection over them. We must pray against rapist, incest, sexual and physical abuse, emotional abuse, including negative words. Declare positive words over them daily and you will see change. Cover them from the attacks of familiar spirits and inappropriate television programs.

Father in the name of Jesus, we come to you right now and we ask that you would put a protection around our children daily from the plans of the enemy. Cover them from attack in out schools, terrorism, rapist witchcraft, sickness in Jesus name. we pray the whole armor of God upon them according to Ephesians 6:18. Bless them and anoint them daily with the spirit of excellence, they will receive honors. Cover them from pedophiles, kidnappers, child labor, pornography, drugs and bad company, social network. We declare that they are blessed and that you will raise them up for times and seasons. We declare wisdom, knowledge and understanding will be their portion and that they will fulfill their purpose and dominate the earth. They will not walk in any attacks of their fathers and forefathers. Grant them favor and scholarships. They will go to the best schools, ivy league schools in Jesus name, Amen.

Chapter 10

MEN AND WOMEN OF PURPOSE ARISE!

Have you ever felt incomplete? Have you ever felt unhappy regardless of what you have accomplished? Have you been feeling restless recently and are getting dreams and visions, some of which you don't understand? Some of you are just going to work for a salary/pay, but there is no joy in what you are doing. Some of you just watch the clock. Some of you have had near death experiences and suffer many things - disappointment, extreme adversities, abuse and even things you don't tell anyone but by yourselves you cry. Many of you have tried to fit in with the boys or girls but it doesn't work. You are different!

When God creates you with greatness inside you, then you must be set apart – you are an eagle, and an eagle does not sit with chickens. That is why you feel odd and incomplete. Even when you have retired, and there is still a fire burning within you, then it means that there is still more within you, and you have not yet fulfilled your purpose!

Each person was created to solve a problem. Many times, when we see chaos, economic problems, injustice, crises with our children – those things come about because the one who was created to deal with that problem is not in proper position. Each time we pray or cry out to God to bring change to an organization or a nation, the answer always lies within a human vessel. That is why Jesus Christ always focused on building the vessel first. God created the earth and equipped it with all He created in it before, then He placed mankind in it. Likewise, He created us – the human vessels – and has equipped us with the solutions within us for the problems that we would encounter.

Within each person is embedded instructions to carry out and when they fail to carry out their assignment, many lives and many things are at stake. Your education is not your purpose, and for many, your job is not your purpose. Some of the clues to your purpose include – the things that make you angry when they happen but bring you great joy when they are addressed or fixed; the things that grieve you.

When you see disorder in society, how do you feel about it? Do you become extremely angry? It indicates that you are a born leader. Leadership is a gift given by God. (Romans 8: 7; Romans 12: 7 – 8) Likewise, teaching is a God-given gift! Now we see why there are so many problems within the education system. Some of the wrong people are in the classrooms.

You Don't Decide Your Purpose

God is the one who decides your purpose! He is the one who places you in the geographical location He wants you to be to fulfill your assignment. When you resist your purpose, painful things occur in your life. That is why we ought to be against abortion; because our purpose is decided before we are conceived. Jeremiah 1 specifically states it. Whether we believe in the existence of God or not does not change that.

There are some people within the nation, whether we like them or not, and regardless of our political affiliation, there is greatness within them and if they fulfill their purpose, great change can come.

Imagine if each person begins to fulfill his/her purpose, what major changes would take place.

Predestined For Purpose

Predestined. Some of us have heard or read this word in the Scriptures before but may not full grasp what it means. Romans 9: 28 – 30 says *"And we know that all things work together for good to those who love God, to those who are the called according to His purpose. For whom He foreknew, He also predestined to be conformed to the image of His Son, that He might be the firstborn among many brethren. Moreover, whom He predestined, these He also called; whom He called, these He also justified; and whom He justified, these He also glorified."* (See also Ephesians 1: 5)

There are times things happen to us for which we never bargained. We may also be disappointed or lacking in joy each day we are in a profession that does not bring us satisfaction, and then we realize that there must be more than where we are. There may be people who are unsaved, or are atheists, or lawmakers determined to put things in place to stop the growth of Christianity. But deep within, they realize that something isn't adding up. You were with Christ from before the foundation of the earth, which means that He wants us to be in His image, walk righteous, holy – believing in the things He believes.

"...For whom He foreknew, He also predestined to be conformed to the image of His Son, that He might be the firstborn among many brethren..." (Romans 8: 29) This tells us that before we were born into this world, we were with Him, made to conform to HIS image. We must align to our true identity – who we were before we were born here. That is why the fight is so great. Only through salvation a spiritual birth – will our eyes be opened so that we can begin walking into what we were predestined to be.

This establishes the fact that God predestined us based on His foreknowledge of us. The word predestined comes from the merging of two Greek words – *"prohorizo"*. *"Pro"* means *"in front"* in a spatial sense or *"before"* in a temporal sense. *"Horizo"* means "to determine or ordain" or *"to appoint."*

You may be in a common-law relationship, being poorly treated; but you are royalty. You may be a janitor, but you were predestined to be wealthier than Bill Gates; or you might have made the mistake of marrying the wrong person. You may be predestined to be a prophet, but you are in the wrong profession. Life and purpose were decided before physical birth, that is why God hates abortion.

Our cemeteries are filled with the remains of people with unfulfilled purpose. Why do you believe people are so angry when it comes to injustice? It may be because God has predestined them to be a lawyer, a judge, or a civil rights leader. What about those who hate to see people sick? Maybe they were predestined to be a doctor, nurse or other health professional, or maybe they have the gift of healing and don't yet know it. There are those who hate to see people poor or lacking necessities of life. They may be predestined to own and operate large humanitarian centers to help the poor.

The Spirit of Prophecy and Word of Knowledge are tools God uses to reveal one's predestined purpose. I have seen people who saw themselves as just another average Joe and when the Lord revealed their purpose/calling they didn't embrace it initially. But the moment they did everything fell into place. I met a lawyer, but the Lord told him "you are the Mayor." He didn't fully embrace it at first, but when he did and ran for office in less than a year, he became the mayor.

We are predestined for greatness with all the **pneumatikos** blessings (Ephesians 1: 1 – 6), that is everything we needed from the foundation of the earth.

1 Corinthians 2: 9 reminds us, *"Eye has not seen, nor ear heard, nor have entered into the heart of man the things which God has prepared for those who love Him."*

There are many within society that are fighting for power, but the question is, are you predestined for that position you are pursuing?

No Fight No Victory

We are in constant fights. We fight for our faith, family, finance, character and even for our purity. We fight the spiritual forces of evil and even to maintain our love for our Saviour. We also must fight to maintain our health and to overcome things like depression, low self-esteem and confidence. But as we go through our daily routine, we cannot afford to succumb. We are in the race and we must not stop until we win that race – whatever it takes. There can be no reward or medal unless you stay in the race. The more fierce the battle is, the greater the reward.

We cannot fight or walk sitting down, and so we are admonished to stand. God says "Stand". Remember that there is no victory without a battle – no winning without the fight, and the greatest fight we are going through right now is the fight within our minds.

Keys To Remember In The Fight

Each day, many wake up asking the questions, "Why am I here? What is my purpose? Who am I? Am I good enough?" The guilt and the condemnation that many battle within the mind and from the past as well as the doubt and unbelief that plagues is often the root of much depression and oppression, but you must fight to rise above it all.

Always remember, the enemy will always attack when you are on the verge of promotion or change. Stop believing the voice that lies, telling you that you are too old, not good enough, and all that. Winston Churchill, late Prime Minister of England never stopped fighting until he became Prime Minister on two occasions – in 1945 after the World War when he was 66 years old and again in 1951, when he was 77 years old.

Never be weary, fearful or faint-hearted when you are in a battle. Remember Deuteronomy 20: 4 which reminds you that God will go before you and fight for you. Recognize that without the lies being told, without the enemies, without your Goliath, you will not get to your destiny. Attacks are inevitable and always come when you are next in line for something big.

Positive Words

Always speak positive words when you are in battle. Your positive confession can determine the outcome of the battle. Stay away from doubters. All men fall but the great ones get up. When you get knocked down don't stay down, you are on the verge of the greatest comeback.

Get to know and remember the story of a boxer named Danny Williams, holder of the British heavyweight title. He made a comeback with one hand – the other was broken and they told him he was finished.

Soccer enthusiasts should never forget Barcelona's comeback – one of the greatest in any championship league.

They came back from four goals down to beat Paris St. Germain. In 2012 Sweden came back and leveled against Germany.

In this 2022 World Cup Soccer, there is much shock and awe as many big names have had to go home including Spain, Mexico, and Germany.

Encourage Yourself

Sometimes in battle you have to encourage yourself. You must see yourself the way God sees you. Not everyone will be there to encourage you. You have to encourage yourself. Never let go of your dreams and visions. You may be broke now, but you are on the verge of your greatest comeback, and all haters and doubters will see your comeback.

Never focus on your battles, your bills, your mountains or how you feel more than the God we serve. There is always something you have in your hands or within your household that will allow you to win the battle.

Never despise small things or small beginnings when you are in a battle. God always allows us to use the small things to defeat big enemies. Your profits, sales and margins may be down, but you are about to come back.

The key during certain seasons of battle is to know the season you are in, and how to operate. Sometimes we have to keep silent or stand still within a season (Exodus 14: 14).

Never forget the story of the Red Sea and Moses. It may seem as if you are on the verge of drowning, but you are about to have the greatest comeback. Remember, you are born to win.

Woman Stand By Your Man

There is a major push globally to undermine and remove our men as head of the nuclear/traditional family model/unit, and it is critical for our women to begin to discern the plans of the enemy that are at work within the society. There are so many things coming against our boys and they are being forsaken and abused within our society. Prisons are being filled with the unrealized potential of our men and boys where it should be harnessed for the betterment of our society.

Divisive strategies are being employed by some women to support and foster this woman-driven move, not because they care about other women, but more so because their main target is to remove any patriarchal reference or symbol from the society and promote a society run by women. How interesting it is though, that some of these women are crying out against the "division" within the society, but instead of promoting healing and unity are purporting continued division between men and women. Could it be that those who propel such action were failed by their own families through, absentee fathers, divorce and so on?

It is critical for our women to stand more forcefully with their men and recognize the trickery. Women need to understand that they were created different from the men. Men were formed out of the ground and women were created out of the men, so they were created differently. That indicates that their functions and ways would be different.

Recognize that the attack against the men, is an attack against God's order and the family. One of the men's roles is to protect the family as it's covering, and another is to be provider.

What Men Should Know

It is no secret that many women say that they can wear any sexy outfit and seduce any man they want to in order to get any document signed in their favor on any issue, including abortion rights, because they know that men often make decisions with them with what is in their underpants rather than what God put in their brains. But men need to wake up and stand up for the God-ordained family.

Men! Wake Up!

Men must recognize that when they make themselves absentee fathers, when they are out of position and out of alignment with God's plan, then our daughters and sons become targets for slaughter and the women are exposed to the attacks from the enemy.

Men cannot be what God did not create them to be, nor should they try to be. Furthermore, as men one of two genders created in the image of God, they are required to embrace everything the Father embraces – doing what He says, being what He says.

Men need to begin to take their place as the priests in their home and in the Church. Women are often more faithful in Spiritual things. When men pray, things change.

Sadly, the men can be found in the swing clubs, strip clubs and many engage in common law relationships which nations now want to streamline as if it is something good.

Men, in order to walk in dominion, you must walk in God's image. (Genesis 1: 26 – 27) You must also show great understanding to our women so that, according to 1 Peter 3: 7, your prayers will not be hindered. Furthermore, you must love your wife as Christ loves the Church. (Ephesians 5: 23 - 25)

Men need to follow the instructions of 1 Corinthians 16: 13 - "Watch, stand fast in the faith, be brave, be strong."

Men must manage their household well and have your children in submission.

While the world evolves, God's word stands. Men must seek to be transformed by renewing their minds daily and staying in relationship with God.

Remember that whenever the enemy wants to go after the family, he will go after the men first and women must recognize this and stand with and for the men and boys. The men are not the enemy in our society.

Women, you must now rise up, spend less time on the social media and invest more time in praying for the victory of the men and the family. Pray that they remain pure and faithful.

Chapter 11

THE DAILY FIGHT MEN GO THROUGH

We are living in a time where men are under constant attack, and it is critical for men to have the right partner to stand with them to bring balance. No man or woman is perfect – perfecting is a process. Many women today would will more readily curse their men rather than pray for them and speak blessings over them.

Women, the main fact that you are chosen to be the queen, it means that God has given you a level of grace to deal with the problems that may arise.

From the beginning of time in the Garden of Eden, Satan has been after the men – the high priests, fathers and husbands – and launched an all-out war on them. The men represent headship, family leadership and the image of God. They are the covering and intercessors for their families. They are the kings who have been given the authority to name and rename things. This is why there is such a fight.

There are many organizations formed to bring men down and to discredit them, destroy their families and some also seek to replace men as the headship of the family – thereby standing against God's original plan for the family.

The spirits of Jezebel and Delilah exist to destroy men by weakening them, and ultimately abort their purpose. Oftentimes, women want men to change to become what they as women want them to be; but women must come to the understanding that men were formed, women were made and so they were created differently. They function differently and their roles are different. Women must begin to pray that the men become who God wants them to become, because they are for His purpose.

Identity Crisis

To be the roof is not easy, because the sun, heat and elements come beating down on it first with great intensity. This is the situation with the men who are the covering for their family.

Many want to change the identity of the men. However, in Genesis 1: 26 – 27, God clearly outlines His plans and blueprint for the human race. What God did not create He does not bless; and what He does not bless will not be fruitful. Our job is to be fruitful, multiply and replenish the earth.

There is great effort being made to control the population globally, and a big part of it includes changing the identity of our men. The males of our species are the carriers of the seed which produces life. He has the word in his mouth, and he can either bless or curse. So, when the men are out of line, the body (the family) suffers.

The Role Of The Men

Contrary to popular belief, a man's function goes beyond producing, transporting and maintaining semen. They are responsible for the total welfare of the family, and he must lead, guide, discipline, protect, provide physically and spiritually for their family and protect them from evil. They must be examples of Godliness, holiness and righteousness.

While most men may provide physically, they fail to provide spiritually. They must ensure that their families walk in obedience to God's Word. A husband who is not faithful to God cannot be faithful to his wife. While the man may have many pitfalls, they must never compare themselves with others.

Most men are broken and have been abandoned by their fathers. Most are fearful of failing to protect and provide for their families. So many have a fear of not living up to expectations. There are some out there who suffer the same abuse as women but society is silent on it. So, it is critical for the women to identify these things and pray against the daily attacks that come against the men. Men need to have faith in God, set their goals and do not quit!

Men, be confident and let your self esteem increase. Look to God to set you free from all bondage. Build your foundation on Him and pray daily. Where your earthly father has abandoned you, your Heavenly Father is always with you and will not leave you. Do not allow society to dictate who you are; instead fulfill the purpose for which God created you.

The Neglect Of Men In Our Society

The decline of the society is the result of the neglect of the men in our society. Our men are hurting because most of them have been physically abused, imprisoned, murdered and unlike our women, there is no outcry for the men when something happens. You will hear people talk about women and children, but they are silent within the society when it comes to men. Billions will be given to empower women – even grants; but nothing when it comes to men.

No nation or society can be successful or prosperous when the men, who carry the seed of life – the covering, the head of the household, the leader of the family are treated that way and are out of position. Where there is no coverage, then our women and children are left to the elements. Before change can come there needs to be alignment within the Body. If the Body is not properly aligned then there will be pain and suffering.

There are many who want to pass laws to shackle our men, but they must remember that there is no earthly law that can change God laws and what He establishes. When real men pray change takes place. When real men speak, things change. God gives men the power to name and to change things. We call upon every virtuous woman to pray for the men and stand with them throughout the nations.

Many will say that our men are the problem, but if you check the root then you would be surprised to see who is at the root. Real women/virtuous women know the value of men within society.

If a nation is serious about reducing crime, poverty, and violence, then drastic measures must be put in place. Feminism was birthed out of the absence of fathers and many of the men are influenced by women, so they fail to take up their responsibility within the home. We cannot continue with a headless generation. God created the men in His image – giving them Godly qualities, intellect, and authority to hear, see, speak, bless and name and the capacity to live holy and righteous, having the characteristics of God. They are the carriers of seed.

God intended to live through men and women and reveal Himself in the world having given mankind His character, authority and image to display His indisputable power over the powers of darkness. The first man and woman were a microcosm of the Church where His glory would manifest in a united and combined effort.

Men are fathers, husbands, providers and protectors of the family unit and since the beginning of time and the enemy has always wanted to divide the men and women. This is why we see laws being passed to diminish the value of the family within society. Real women don't get involved in gender fights; they know the value of the men in their lives.

If we are serious about crime and violence, then alignment has to take place. When the neck becomes the head then darkness takes dominion and results in crime, violence and lawlessness. It is for that reason each man must use his body as an image of righteousness. He must therefore flee:

- ✓ Sexual immorality/Perversion
- ✓ Gambling
- ✓ Abandonment of their families for other women
- ✓ Drugs
- ✓ Drunkenness
- ✓ Idolatry
- ✓ Witchcraft

When a nation struggles, it indicates that there is a lack of real men. When the children murder or are murdered it is a sign of the absence and neglect of our men within the society. That is why the church, the civil society, as well as private and public entities and individuals need to give all the support to empower, encourage and edify our men if they want to see change. The men are forgotten by a society that chooses to build them prisons instead of schools, meanwhile the same society advocates prostitution instead of real and viable solutions.

- ✓ **Real men stand with their children regardless of their status. They are not easily manipulated by Delilah and Jezebel.**

- ✓ **Real Men lead from the front instead of allowing their lower extremities to influence their decision-making. They look to God as their source and for strength.**

- ✓ **Real men speak life and encouragement to their families and communities.**

Let us make every effort to rescue our boys and help them to become real men just as King Lemuel's mother did for him. It is time to honor, value and respect our men.

Chapter 12

WISDOM FOR HEALTHY LIVING

Always remember Jeremiah 29: 11 – you can have many plans but is it the Lord's plan. It is God's plan that counts, and it is His plan that will come to pass. The question is, do we just make a plan, or do we just seek God for His plan for our lives?

Proverbs 21: 2 further reminds us that, *"Every way of a man is right in his own eyes, but the Lord weighs the hearts."* Everybody believes that they are right in the things they do, how they live and so on. But the Lord searches thoroughly through man's heart to see that his motives are right and his heart is clean according to His standards, principles and way.

Proverbs 20: 21 says, *"An inheritance gained hastily at the beginning will not be blessed at the end."* Many are creating their "blessing" and refuse to wait for the will of God to manifest in their lives. The quick schemes and shortcuts through the process will bring pain in the end.

Psalm 37: 37 says *"Mark the blameless man and observe the upright; For the future of that man is peace."* Not because something feels right does it necessarily mean it is right; and if any "peace" you have about it does not come through God's Word on the matter, then it is not God.

Proverbs 27: 2 *"Let another man praise you, and not your own mouth; a stranger, and not your own lips."* This speaks for itself and needs no explanation.

Proverbs 29: 23 tells us: *"A man's pride will bring him low, but the humble in spirit will retain honor."* and Psalms 138: 6 *"Though the Lord is on high, yet He regards the lowly; but the proud He knows from afar."* Humility is the key to prosperity. Stay humble always. Humility is not a weakness.

Deuteronomy 8: 18, *"And you shall remember the Lord your God, for it is He who gives you power to get wealth, that He may establish His covenant which He swore to your fathers, as it is this day."* Success takes more than gifts, talents and education. In order to walk in true prosperity, it takes God's Favor and Grace.

Take not of Numbers 20: 8 – 12. Always seek the approval of God before the blessing of God. Many have the blessings but don't have the approval. Never forget Moses, he struck the rock when he should have spoken to it as instructed. He got the blessings of God – the water – but he didn't get the approval from God to do it the way he did, and he did not get approved to enter the Land of Promise. The approval and the blessings are different. God can bless you with the house, but He didn't approve that one for you, so He won't live in it with you.

Habakkuk 2: 2 – 3 says, 2 Then the Lord answered me and said: "Write the vision and make it plain on tablets, that he may run who reads it. For the vision is yet for an appointed time; but at the end it will speak, and it will not lie. Though it tarries, wait for it; because it will surely come, it will not tarry." Every vision has a process before it comes to full manifestation. The manifestation can take years. Make the first step and write the vision down.

Problems Are Temporary

Problems are everywhere and there are times problems are the order of the day. Hardship, job loss, betrayal, disappointment, sickness, financial problem, relationship problems, divorce, threat of exposure, and blackmail are real and many are falling under pressure. When it seems as if there is no way out of your situation, the enemy always tries to convince a person that suicide is the best option for you and that by taking your own life the problem will be solved. **That Is Not So!** That is deception. Committing suicide means your problems have just begun. There is no repentance in the grave. Hebrews 9: 27 says, *"And as it is appointed for men to die once, but after this the judgment."*

We must recognize that during problems there is always a way. So, when problems overwhelm us, we must give Him the burdens. As 1 Peter 5: 7 says, "casting all your care upon Him, for He cares for you." One meaning for the word "cast" is "the act of throwing something forcefully." So, throw your problems to the Lord, because He is ready to take your yoke and your heavy burden. (Matthew 11: 28)

When problems come, He wants us to seek Him in all things. (Matthew 6: 33) Many fail to seek God for solutions, they prefer to seek the wrong source that would create greater problem. Know that, in the midst of problems, Prayer and Fasting work! Furthermore, there are other keys of wisdom in the Holy Bible that work. You can also seek anointed women or men of God who will help you to walk through the problem.

Oftentimes the enemy convinces people that the problem is too personal and private to ask anyone for help. **Reject that thought, it is a lie!!!**

Remember that every problem has an expiration date, and that just by reading this article by faith, this may be the very date your problem expires.

Quite often people get attacked when they are on the verge of something great; and that is where you will hear his voice the loudest.

Always remember, whatever you have lost, God can restore in a moment. Never forget Job. There is Job chapter 1, but there is also Job chapter 42.

God is the God of Restoration, and He will give us double for our trouble.

If your spouse walks away, God will give you better.

If you lose your job, God will give you better.

There is no material thing that is greater or of more value than your life. So, why take your life. Always think of those who are depending on you; those looking for your continued help and support. You may not think your life is of any value, or that you are not positively contributing to anything, but that is when your life is making an impact to many others around you.

The Power of Prophecy

The gift of Prophecy is one of the 9 Gifts of the Holy Spirit, and it can be used to bring deliverance in times of problem. Nothing is wrong with seeking a Word of Prophecy that will bring encouragement, edification, and blessing. This gift can give you directions to solve your problems. The breaking of curses gives hope, brings healing. Never forget King Hezekiah, and how God used it to bring healing and longevity.

God's servants are anointed to speak a word of prophecy that can bring down any obstacle in your path, plant new things and can also be used as a time clock of end time events.

Remember, there are many resources in the Kingdom including Word of Knowledge and Word of Wisdom that God will use to help us when we are facing a crisis. Hence, your situation may not be as bad as you think. Embrace life and cancel suicide. You are next in line for your blessing!

The Blessing Prayer

Read 3 times daily before or after meals. (Scriptures to read: Genesis 3: 13 – 14; Genesis 12: 3; Deuteronomy 28: 1 – 14)

Father in the name of Jesus
I come to you right now
And I decree and declare that
I am blessed.
My mind is blessed.
My body is blessed.
I am blessed in the city.
I am blessed in the field.
I am blessed in my going out.
I am blessed coming in.
I decree that my family is blessed.
My marriage is blessed.
My children are (child is) blessed.
My basket is blessed.
My kneading bowl is blessed.
My bank account is blessed.
My house is blessed.
My vehicle is blessed.
All my assets are blessed.
My business is (businesses are) blessed.
Everything I touch is blessed.
My work is blessed.
My workplace is blessed.
My staff is blessed.
My church is blessed.
My leaders are blessed.
My community is blessed.

My children's schools are blessed.
Wherever my feet touch is blessed.
I have the blessing of Abraham on my life,
And through me nations of the earth shall be blessed.
And all the Glory belongs to You Lord,
In Jesus' name I pray. Amen.

Bibliography

Hagee, John C. General Editor, Prophecy Study Bible, (New King James Version) © 1997 Thomas Nelson, Inc

Hayford, Jack W. Executive Editor, New Spirit-Filled Life® Bible, (New King James Version) © 2002 Thomas Nelson, Inc.

Lyston, Steve, Man, Money, Ministry, © 2009 Xlibris

Pfeiffer, Charles F., Vos, Howard F., Rea, John. Editors, Wycliffe Bible Dictionary, (Seventh Printing) © 2005 Hendrickson Publishers, Inc

Strong, James. The New Strong's Expanded Exhaustive Concordance of the Bible, (Red Letter Edition) © 1990 Thomas Nelson Publishers

Concise Oxford English Dictionary Eleventh Edition. © 1964, 1976, 1982, 1990, 1995, 1999, 2001, 2004 Oxford University Press. All Rights Reserved.

www.ingramcontent.com/pod-product-compliance
Lightning Source LLC
Chambersburg PA
CBHW061649040426
42446CB00010B/1653